RECORDED VERSIONS
GUITAR

AUTHENTIC TRANSCRIPTIONS
WITH NOTES AND TABLATURE

Good Charlotte
THE CHRONICLES OF
LIFE AND DEATH

Music transcriptions by Pete Billmann, Addi Booth, Ryan Maziarz and Paul Pappas

ISBN 0-634-09515-3

HAL•LEONARD®
CORPORATION

7777 W. BLUEMOUND RD. P.O. BOX 13819 MILWAUKEE, WI 53213

In Australia Contact:
Hal Leonard Australia Pty. Ltd.
4 Lentara Court
Cheltenham, Victoria, 3192 Australia
Email: ausadmin@halleonard.com

Visit Hal Leonard Online at
www.halleonard.com

D1227820

The Chronicles of Life & Death

Words and Music by Benji Madden and Joel Madden

F5

Tune down 1/2 step:
(low to high) E♭-A♭-D♭-G♭-B♭-E♭

Intro
Moderate Rock ♩ = 146

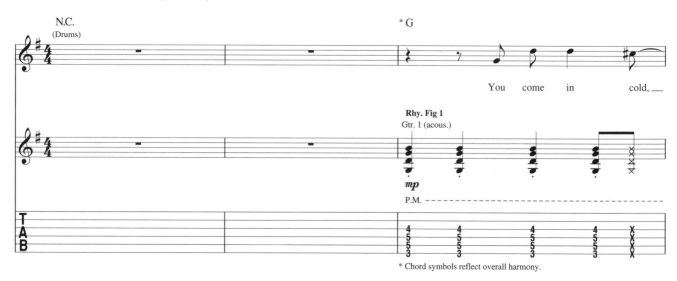

* Chord symbols reflect overall harmony.

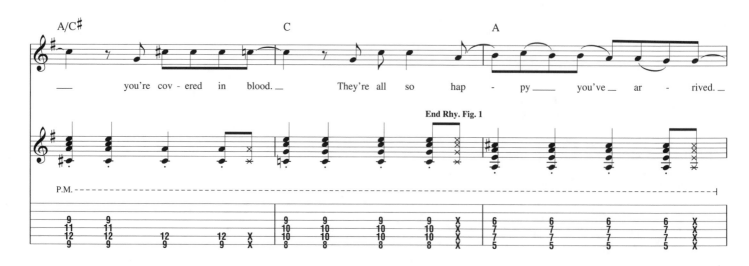

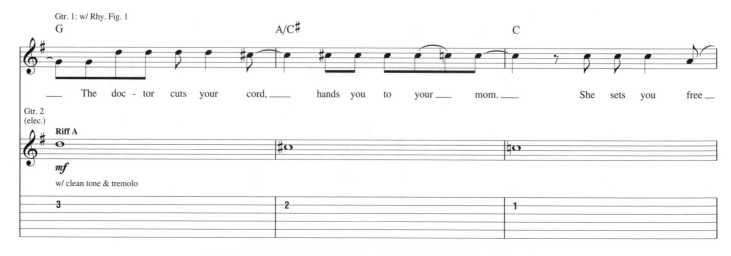

Walk Away (Maybe)

Words and Music by Benji Madden and Joel Madden

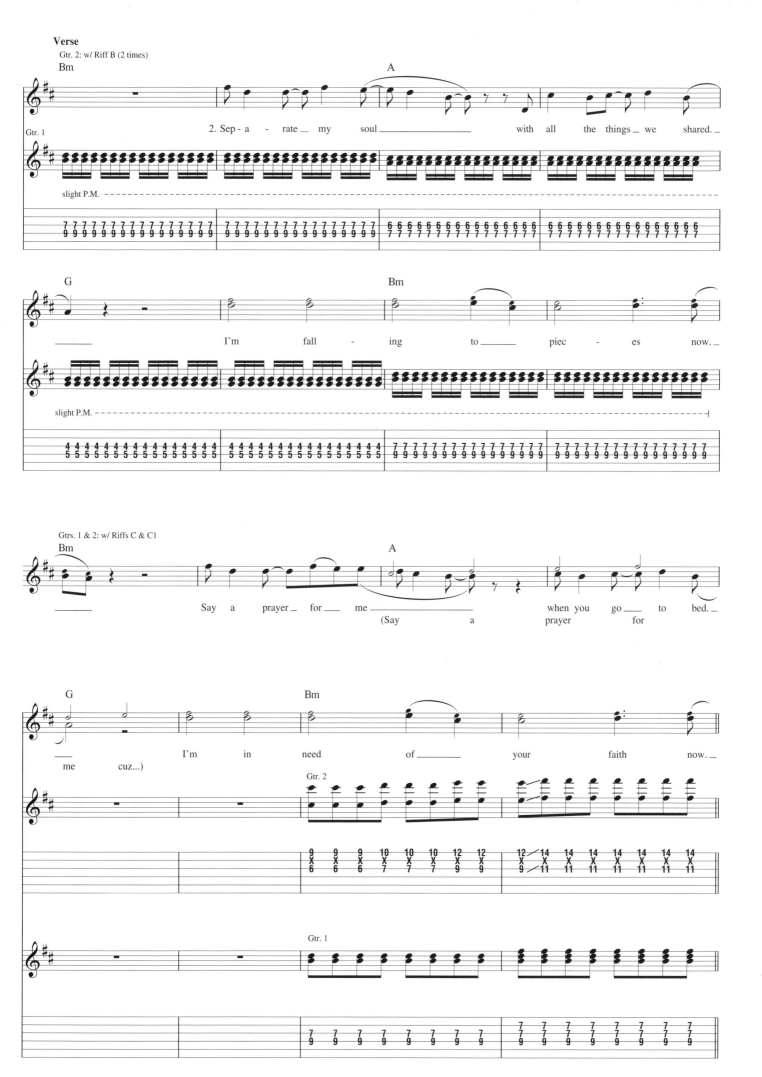

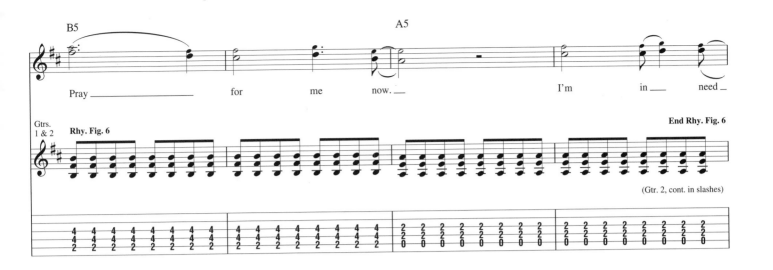

S.O.S.

Words and Music by Benji Madden and Joel Madden

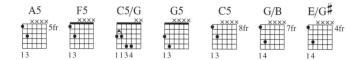

Tune down 1/2 step:
(low to high) Eb-Ab-Db-Gb-Bb-Eb

Chorus
Moderately slow ♩ = 84

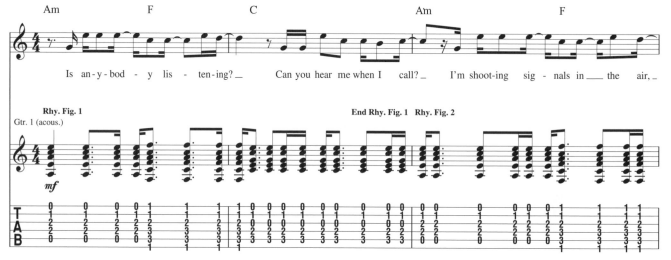

Is an-y-bod-y lis-ten-ing? __ Can you hear me when I call? __ I'm shoot-ing sig-nals in __ the air,

__ 'cause I need some-bod-y's help. __ I can't make __ it on __ my own, __ so I'm giv-ing up __ my - self. __

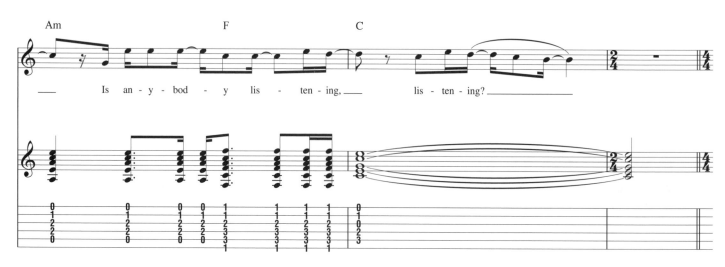

__ Is an-y-bod - y lis - ten-ing, __ lis - ten - ing? _____

Verse
Much faster ♩ = 176

Gtr. 1 tacet

*Fmaj7sus2   Gsus2   Am7sus2

1. I've been strand - ed here _ and I'm miles a - way, _

Riff A
Gtr. 2 (elec.)

mf
w/ dist.
P.M.

Gtr. 3 (elec.)

mf
w/ clean tone & chorus

*Chord symbols reflect implied harmony.

Csus2   G/B   Fmaj7sus2

mak - ing sig - nals, hop - ing they save _____ me. _____

P.M.

End Riff A

mf
let ring

Gtr. 2: w/ Riff A   Gsus2   Am7sus2

I lock my - self _ in - side _ these walls, _ 'cause out there _ I'm al - ways wrong. _

Gtr. 3

let ring   *let ring*

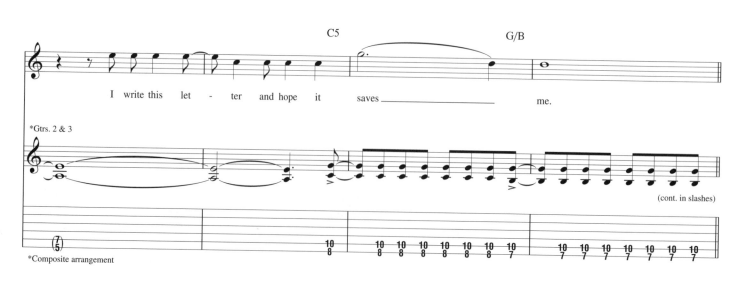

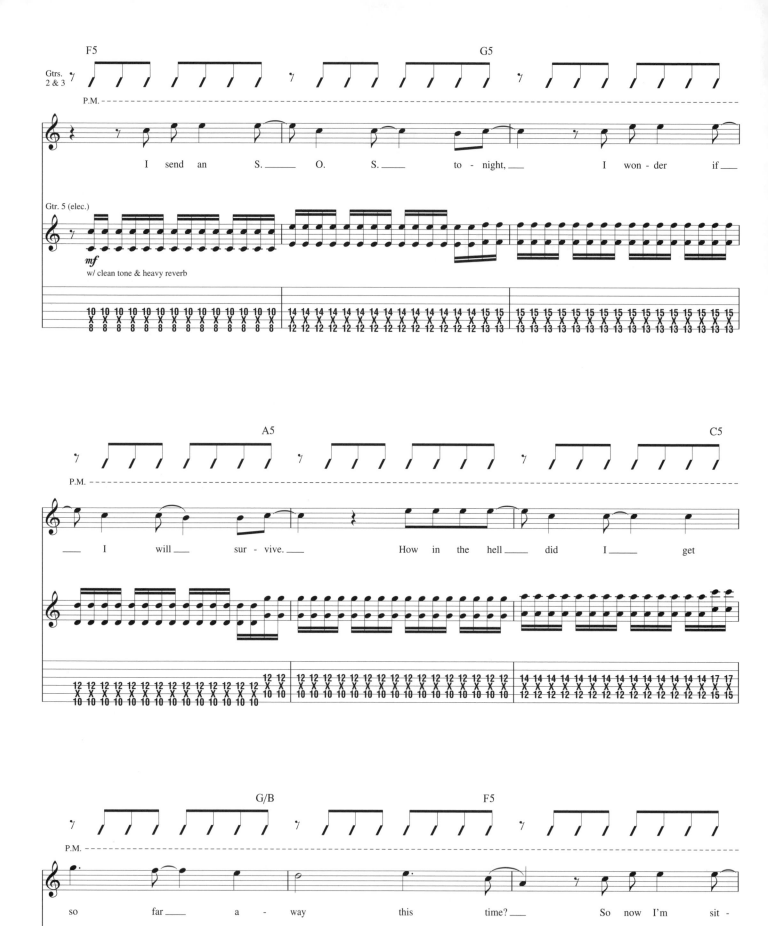

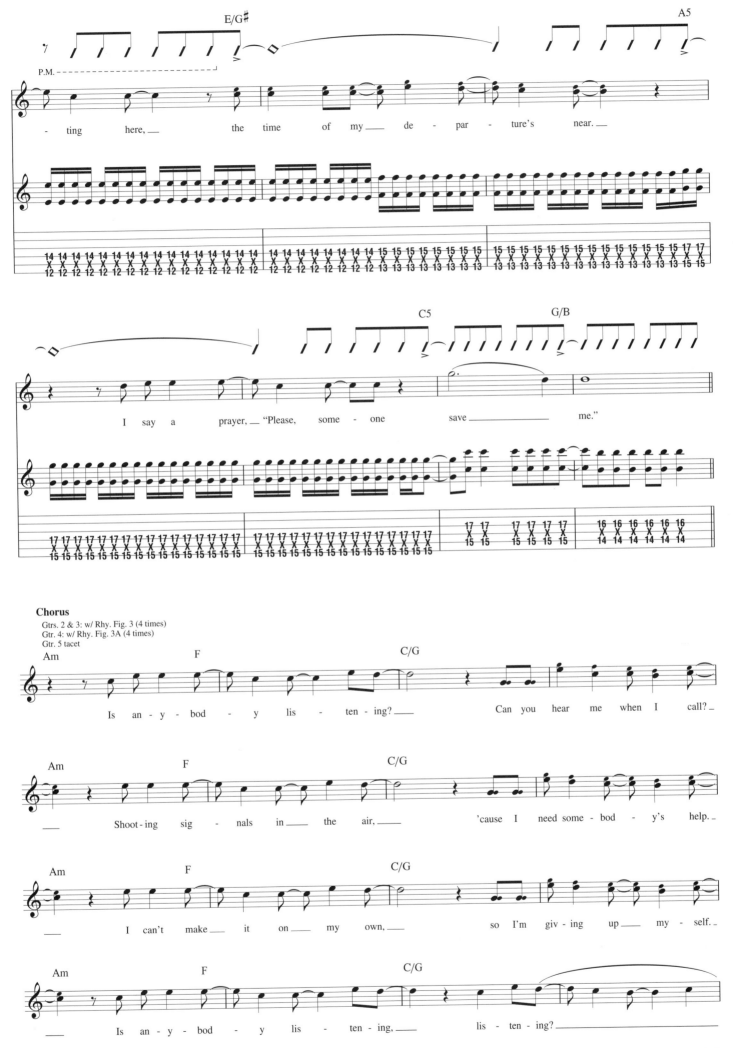

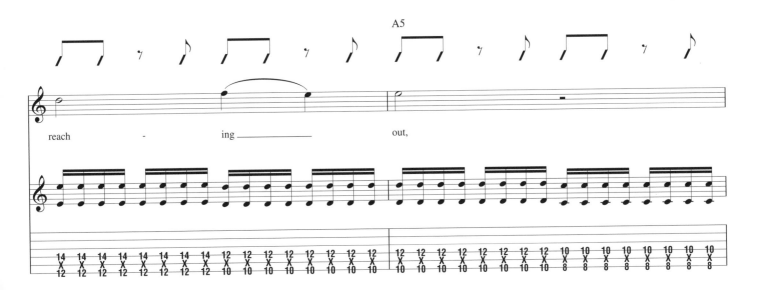

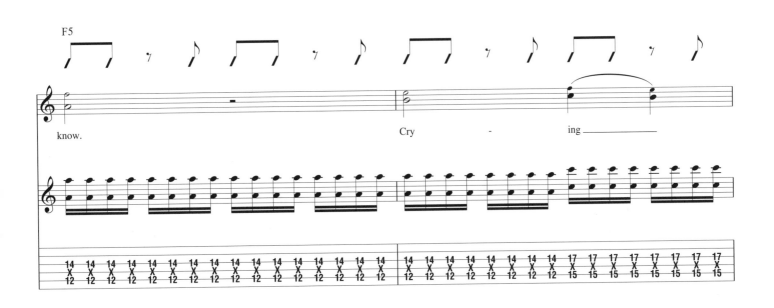

Guitar Solo

Outro-Chorus
Tempo I

Gtr. 1: w/ Rhy. Fig. 1

Gtr. 1: w/ Rhy. Fig. 2 (2 times)
Gtr. 4 tacet

Is an-y-bod-y lis-ten-ing? ___ Can you hear me when I call? ___ Shoot-ing sig-nals in ___ the air, ___

Gtrs. 2 & 3 tacet

___ I need some-bod-y's help. ___ I can't make ___ it on ___ my own, ___ I'm giv-ing up ___ my-self. ___

___ Is an-y-bod-y lis-ten-ing? ___

I Just Wanna Live

Words and Music by Benji Madden, Joel Madden and John Feldmann

Tune down 1/2 step:
(low to high) E♭-A♭-D♭-G♭-B♭-E♭

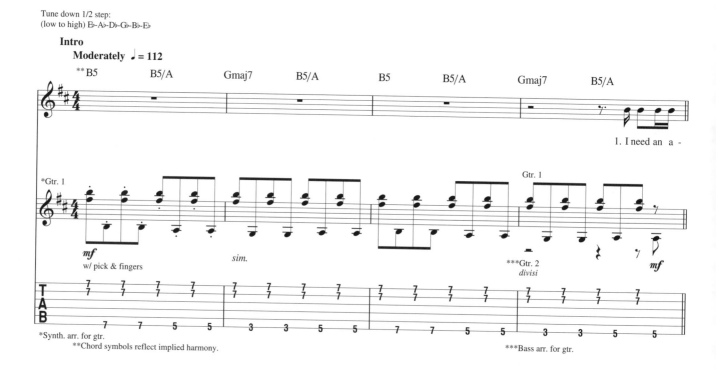

*Synth. arr. for gtr.
  **Chord symbols reflect implied harmony.
  ***Bass arr. for gtr.

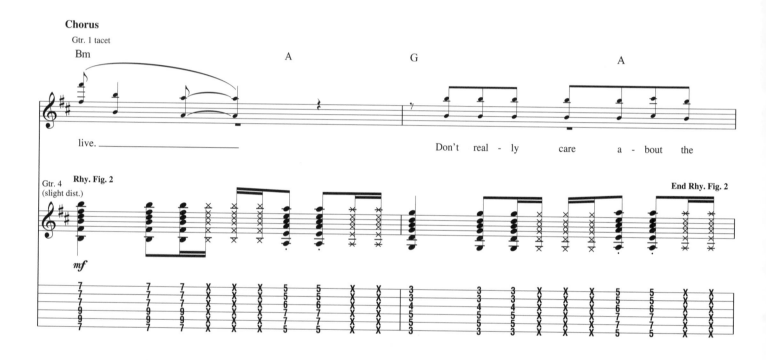

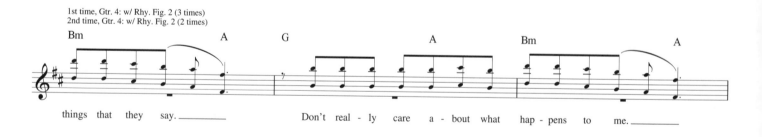

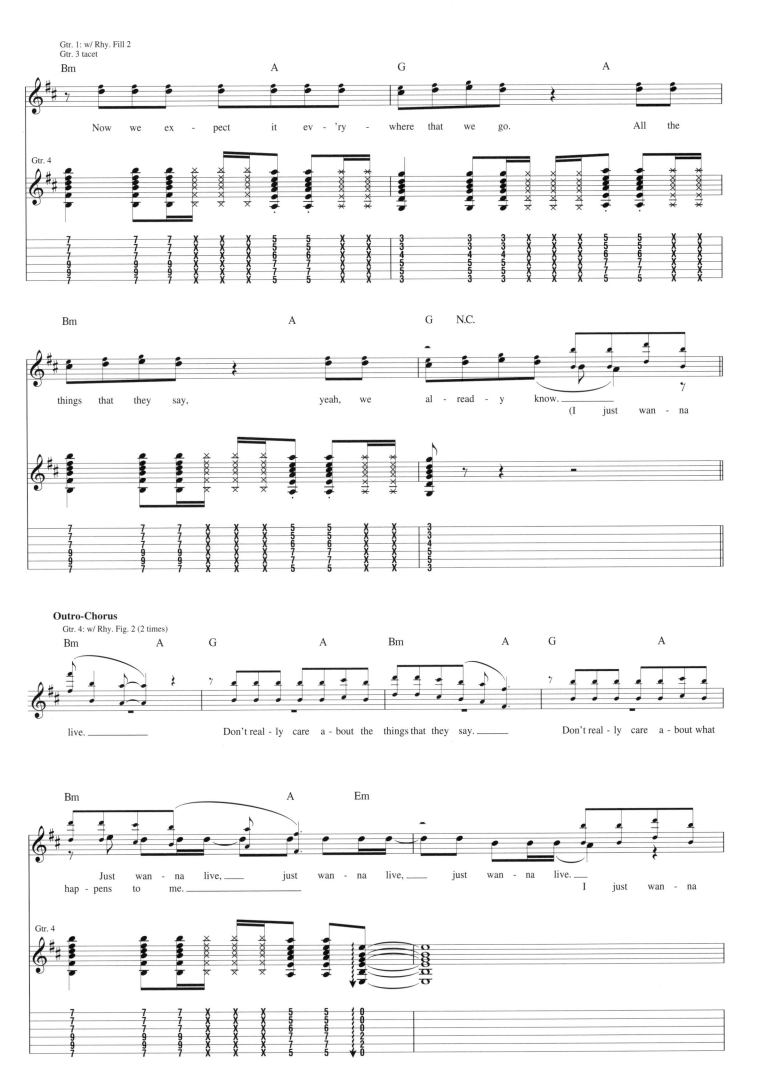

Ghost of You

Words and Music by Benji Madden, Joel Madden and Billy Martin

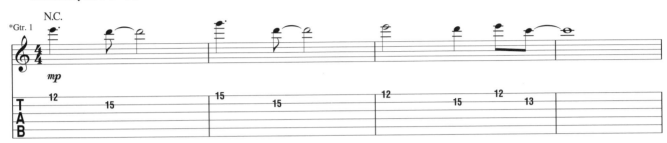

Tune down 1/2 step:
(low to high) E♭-A♭-D♭-G♭-B♭-E♭

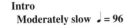

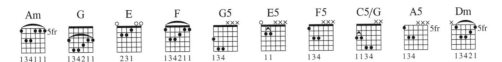

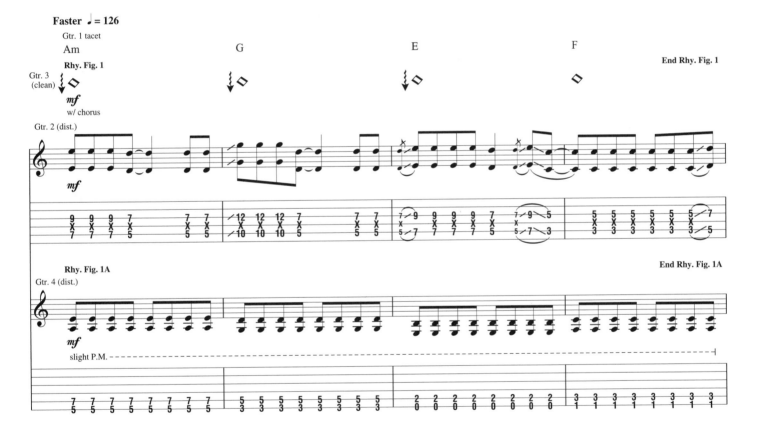

Verse

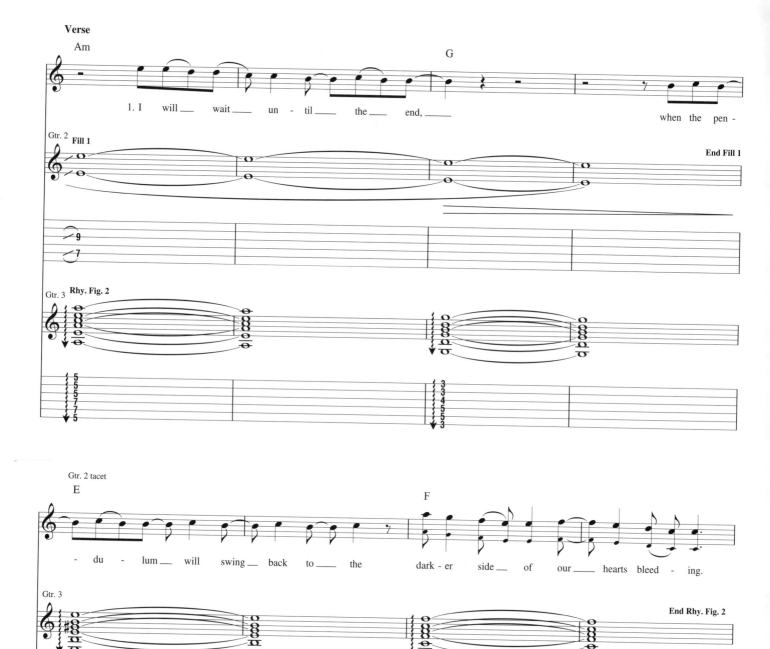

1. I will ___ wait ___ un - til ___ the ___ end, ___ when the pen -

- du - lum ___ will swing ___ back to ___ the dark - er side ___ of our ___ hearts bleed - ing.

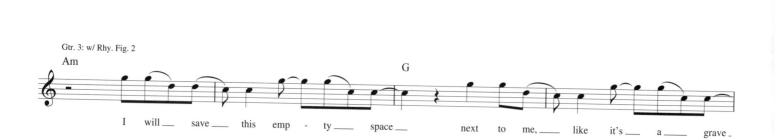

I will ___ save ___ this emp - ty ___ space ___ next to me, ___ like it's ___ a ___ grave ___

___ where I lay ___ a place ___ for us ___ to sleep ___ e - ter - nal - ly ___ to - geth -

wonder - ing __ if it's you __ that I feel, __ if it's you __ that I feel __ here, haunt - ing __ me __ for - ev -

And I'm not look - ing for __ an - y - thing __ but us, __

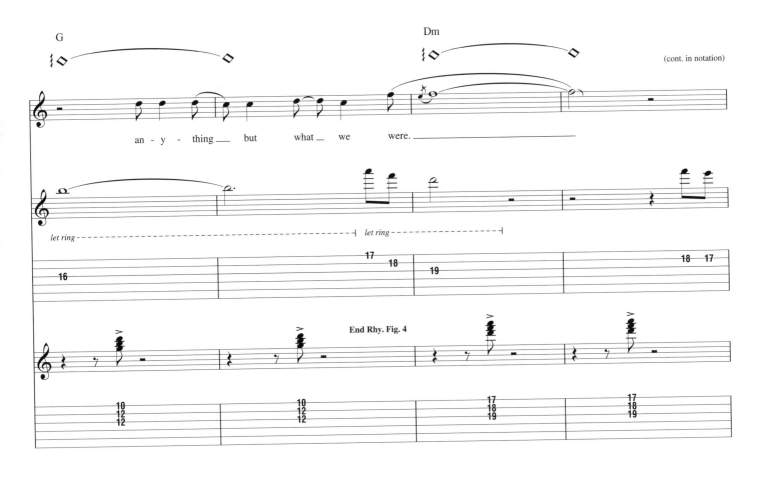

an - y - thing___ but   what___ we   were._____

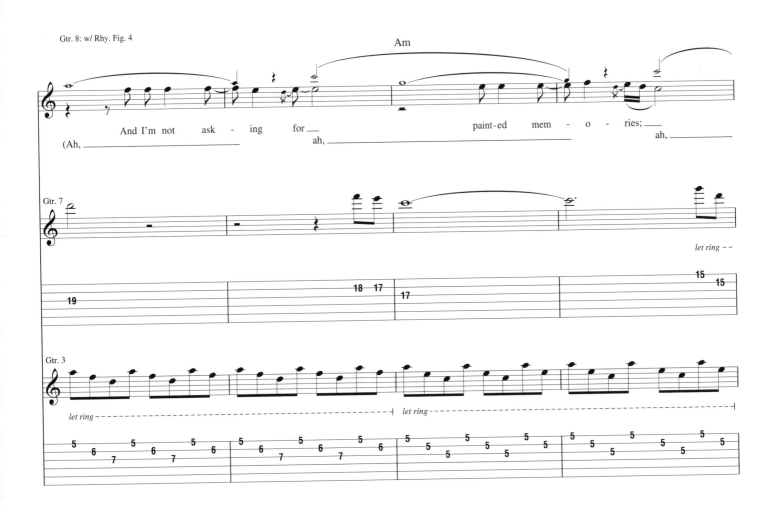

Gtr. 8: w/ Rhy. Fig. 4

And I'm not   ask - ing   for___   paint-ed   mem - o - ries;___
(Ah,_____   ah,   ah,___

Gtr. 7

Gtr. 3

Outro-Chorus

*Gtr. 1: w/ Riff C (3 3/4 times)
*Gtrs. 4 & 5: w/ Rhy. Fig. 3 (3 3/4 times)

Gtrs. 3 & 7 tacet

*Last 1 3/4 times, Gtrs. 1, 4 & 5 gradually fade out.

Predictable

Words and Music by Benji Madden and Joel Madden

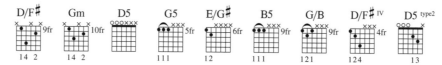

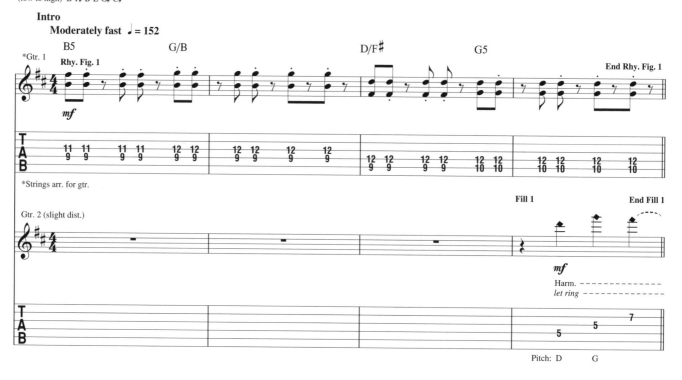

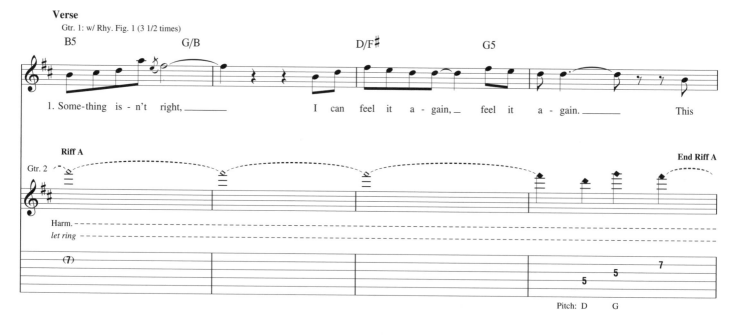

es and false hopes ___ high. _____ I saw this ___ com-

-ing, still I don't know ___ why I let you in. _____
(Ah.) _____

Chorus

I knew it all a- long, ___ it's so pre-dict-a-ble. ___

*Doubled throughout

**Applies to up-stemmed part only.

***Applies to up-stemmed part only.

45

46

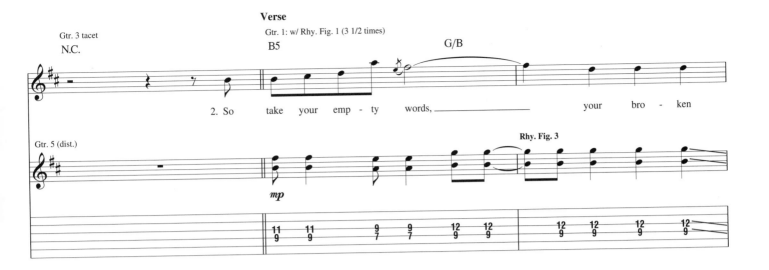

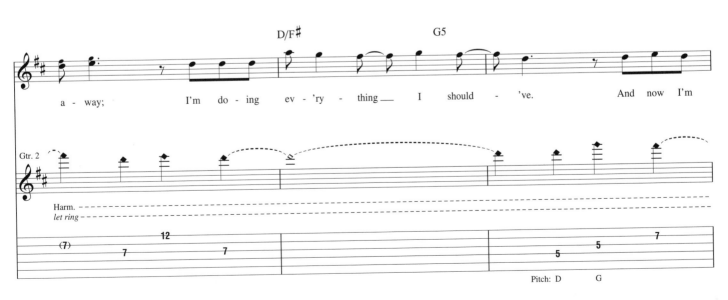

Gtr. 3: w/ Rhy. Fig. 4

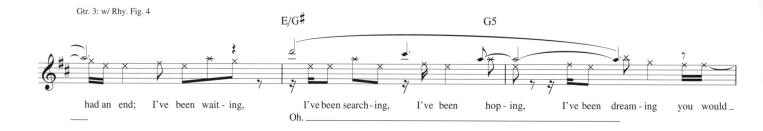

had an end;   I've been wait - ing,   I've been search-ing,   I've been   hop - ing,   I've been dream - ing   you would__
__   Oh._____

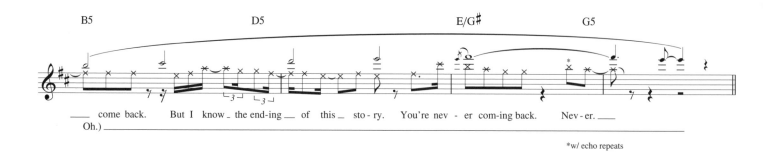

__ come back.   But I know _ the end-ing __ of   this _ sto - ry.   You're nev - er com-ing back.   Nev - er. ___
Oh.)   __

*w/ echo repeats

Interlude

Gtr. 3 tacet

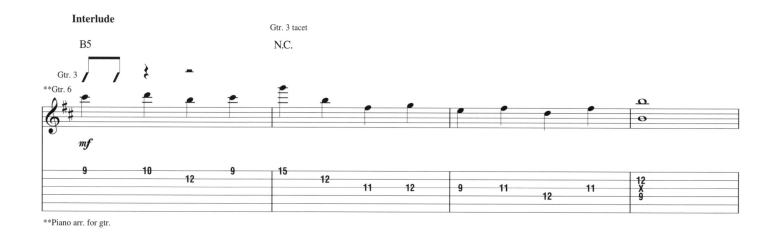

**Piano arr. for gtr.

***Applies to 1st string only.

⊕ **Coda**

Yelled: Ev - 'ry - where I go for the rest _____ of my life, ev - 'ry -

*Bkgd. Voc.: w/ Voc. Fig. 3

one I love, ___ ev - 'ry - one I care a - bout, you're all gon - na want to know what's wrong __

*Top voice only.

Bkgd. Voc.: w/ Voc. Fig. 3

__ with me ___ and I know what it is. I'm end - ing this right now.

(cont. in slashes)

Outro

51

Secrets

Words and Music by Benji Madden and Joel Madden

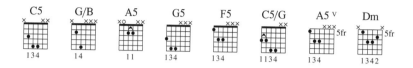

Tune down 1/2 step:
(low to high) E♭-A♭-D♭-G♭-B♭-E♭

Intro

Moderately fast ♩ = 152

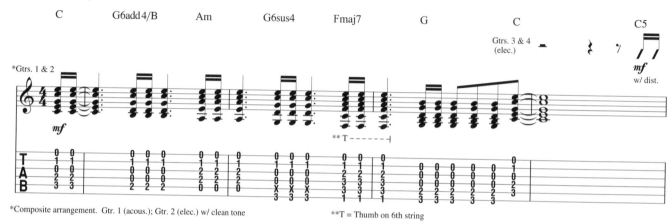

*Composite arrangement. Gtr. 1 (acous.); Gtr. 2 (elec.) w/ clean tone

**T = Thumb on 6th string

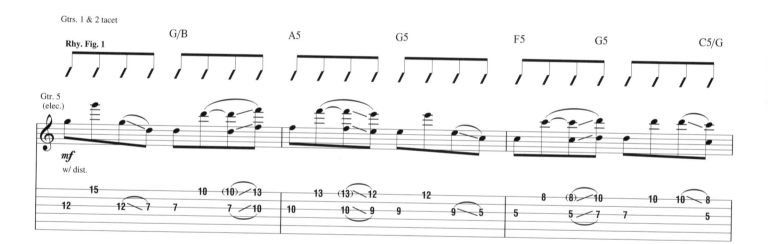

Chorus

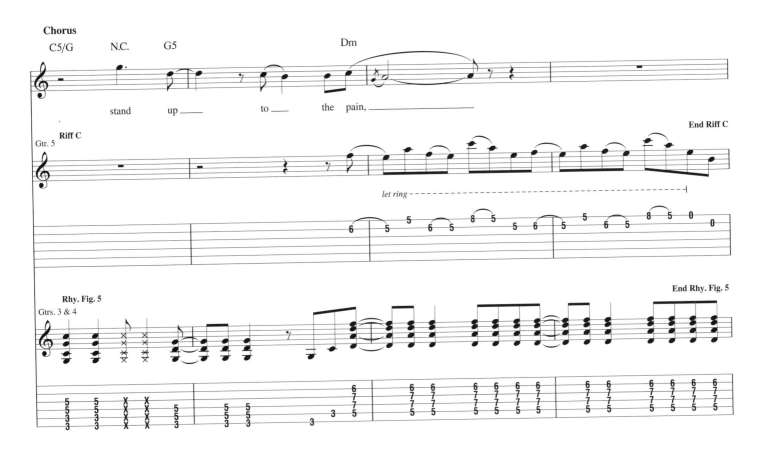

stand up ___ to ___ the pain, ____

2nd time, Gtrs. 3 & 4: w/ Rhy. Fill 2

wake up ___ and fight ___ a - gain. ___ If you could ___

1st time, Gtr. 5: w/ Riff C (2 times)
2nd time, Gtr. 5: w/ Riff C (1 3/4 times)
C5/G N.C. G5 Dm
dance with me through this rain. And we will fight.
Gtrs. 3 & 4
1st time, Gtrs. 3 & 4: w/ Rhy. Fig. 5
2nd time, Gtrs. 3 & 4: w/ Rhy. Fig. 5 (1st 3 meas.)
To Coda
C5/G N.C. G5 Dm
We will fight a - gain, fight a - gain.
Interlude
Gtrs. 3 & 4: w/ Rhy. Fig. 2
Gtr. 5: w/ Riff A
Gtr. 2: w/ Fill 1
C5 G/B A5 G5 F5 G5 C5/G
2. In the back,
Verse
Gtr. 2: w/ Riff B
*Gtr. 6: w/ Rhy. Fig. 3
F5 A5
in the clos - ets of your mind, that's where
*Played mf w/o vol. swells.
F5 C5
skel - e - tons and dirt - y se - crets hide. And I'll
Gtr. 4: w/ Rhy. Fig. 4
F5 A5
rip out my in - sides and
D.S. al Coda
F5 G5
leave them on dis - play for you to - night. 'Cause

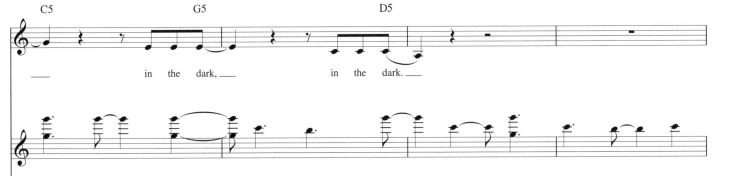

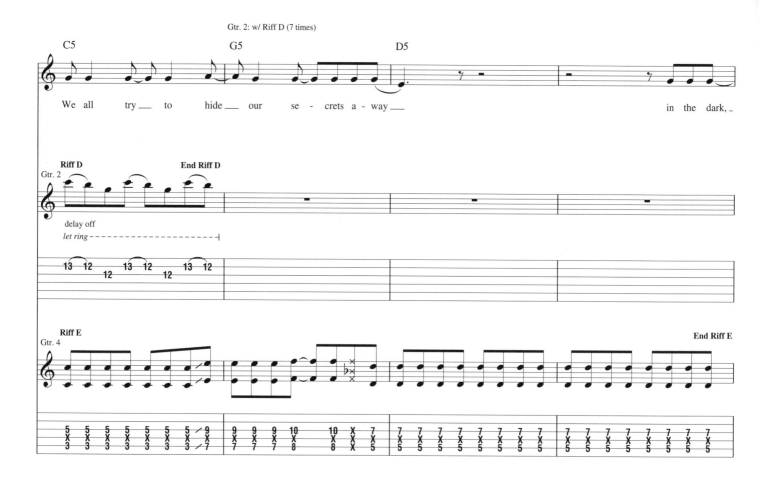

Gtr. 2: w/ Riff D (7 times)

C5   G5   D5

We all try — to hide — our se - crets a - way —   in the dark,

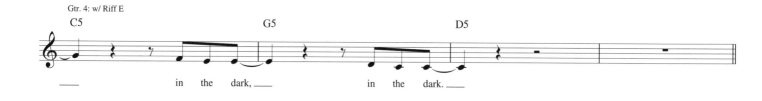

Gtr. 4: w/ Riff E

C5   G5   D5

— in the dark, — in the dark. —

Chorus

Gtr. 5: w/ Riff C (2 times)

C5/G   N.C.   G5   N.C.   Dm

Stand up — to — the pain, ——

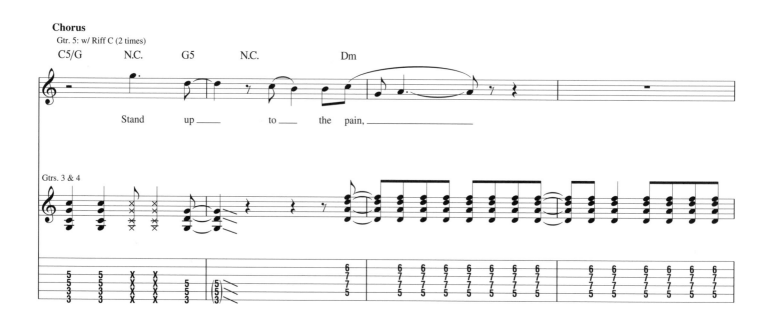

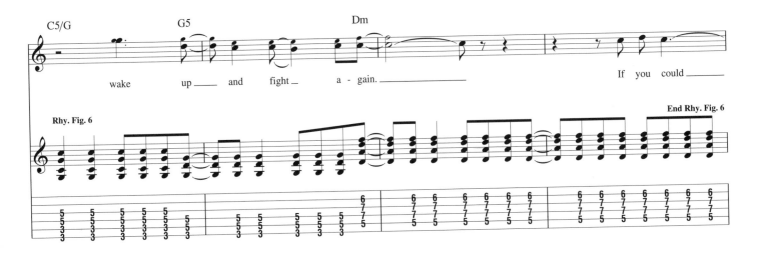

The Truth

Words and Music by Benji Madden, Joel Madden and John Feldmann

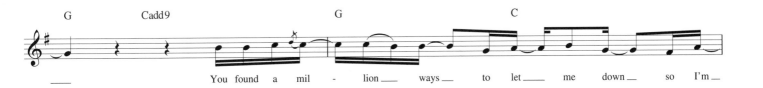

You found a mil - lion ways to let me down so I'm

not hurt when you're not a - round. I was blind, but now I

Pre-Chorus
Gtr. 1: w/ Rhy. Fig. 2

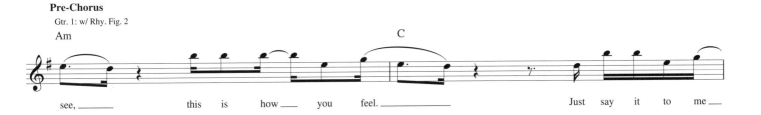

see, this is how you feel. Just say it to me

D.S. al Coda

if this was ev - er real. I want the truth

Gtr. 1

Coda

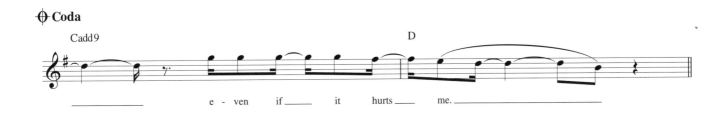

e - ven if it hurts me.

Bridge

I know that this ___ will break ___ me. I know that this ___ might make ___

___ me cry. ___ You got-ta say ___ what's on _____ your ___ mind, _ on ___ your mind. _____

___ I know that this ___ will hurt ___ me and break my heart _ and soul ___ in - side. _ I don't want _ to live _

Chorus

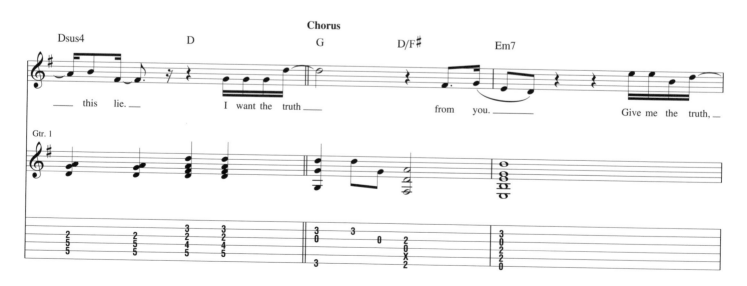

___ this lie. ___ I want the truth ___ from you. _____ Give me the truth, ___

Gtr. 1: w/ Rhy. Fig. 3 (last 2 meas.)

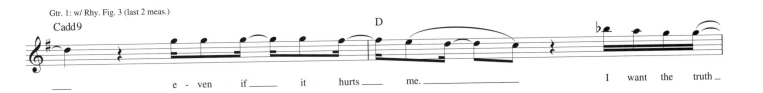

e - ven if ____ it hurts ____ me. _____ I want the truth ____

Gtr. 1: w/ Rhy. Fig. 3 (3 times)

_____ from you. _____ Give me the truth, ___ e - ven if __ it hurts. __

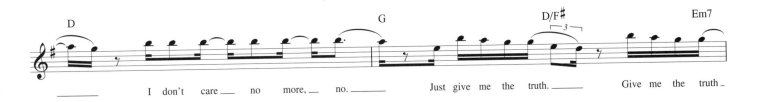

_____ I don't care __ no more, __ no. _____ Just give me the truth. _____ Give me the truth __

_____ 'cause I don't care __ no __ more. __ Give me the truth ____ 'cause I don't _ care _ no more, _ no. _____

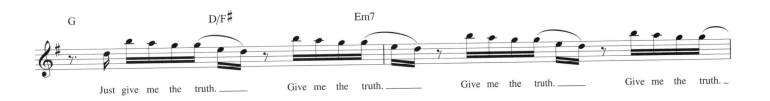

Just give me the truth. _____ Give me the truth. _____ Give me the truth. _____ Give me the truth. __

_____ Give me the truth _____ 'cause I don't care __ no more, _ no.

Outro

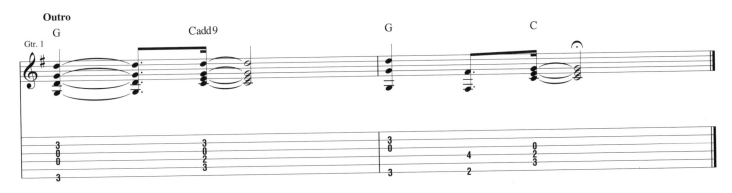

The World Is Black

Words and Music by Benji Madden and Joel Madden

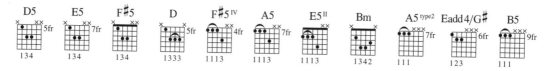

Drop D tuning, down 1/2 step:
(low to high) Db-Ab-Db-Gb-Bb-Eb

Moderately fast ♩ = 157

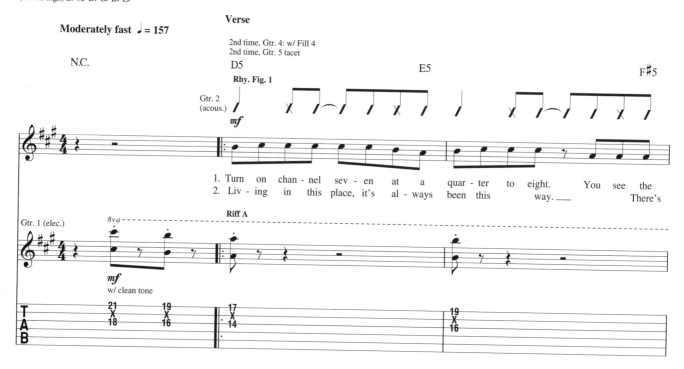

1. Turn on chan-nel sev-en at a quar-ter to eight. You see the
2. Liv-ing in this place, it's al-ways been this way. ___ You see the There's

same damn thing, it's just a dif-fer-ent ___ day. ___ And no one real-ly knows ___
no one do-ing noth-ing, so there's noth-ing changed. _ And I can't live ___ when this ___

Fill 4
Gtr. 4

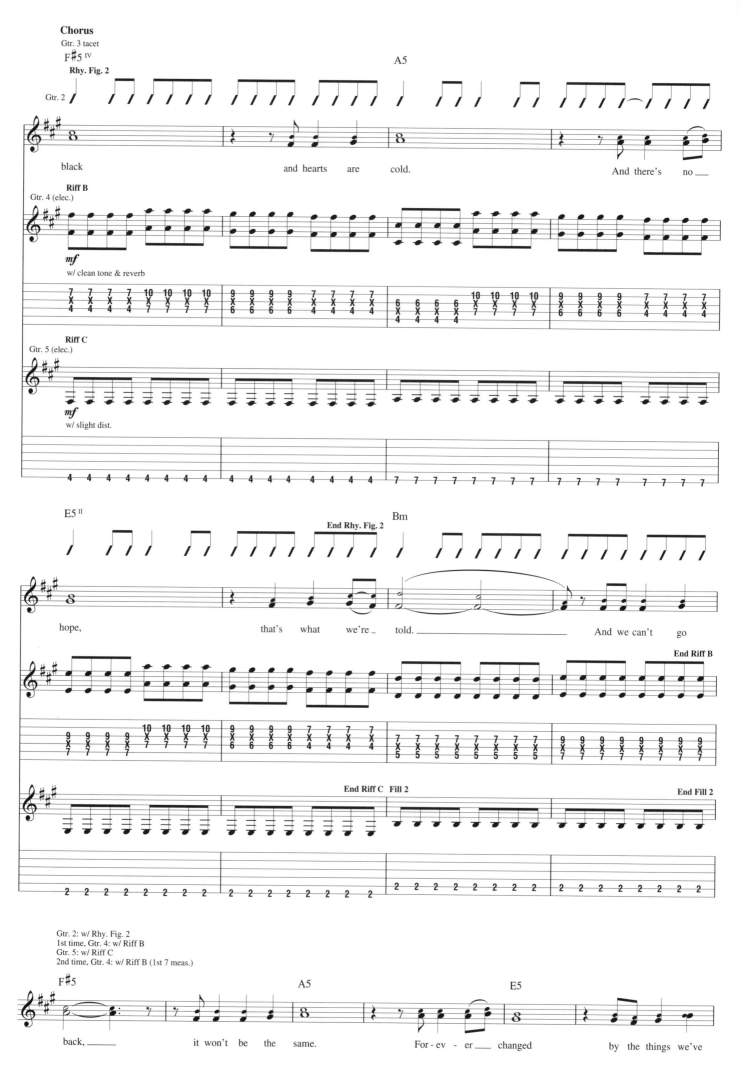

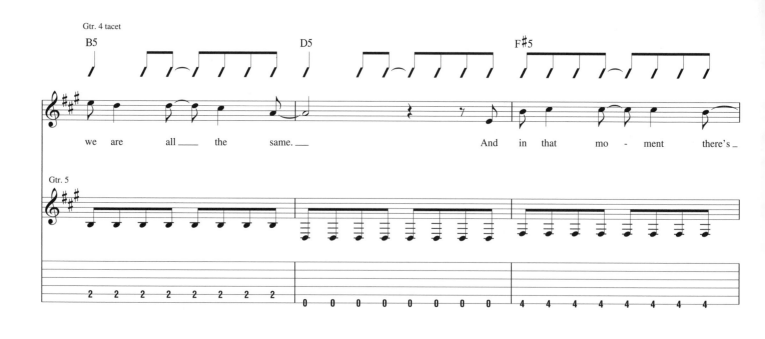

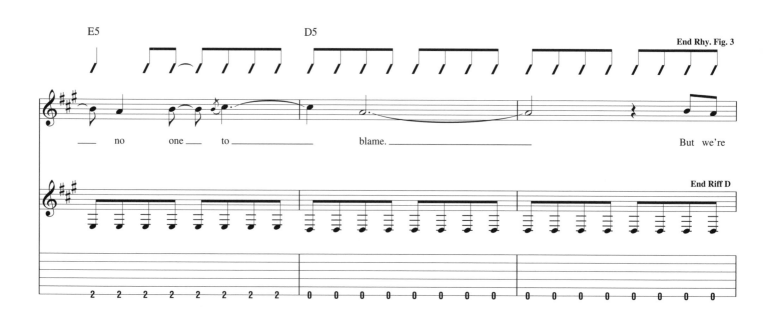

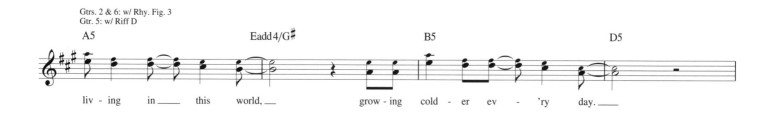

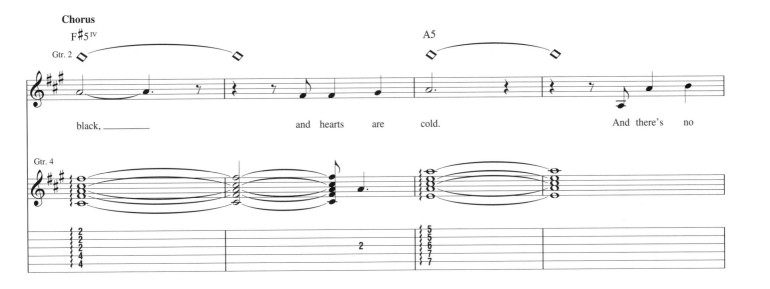

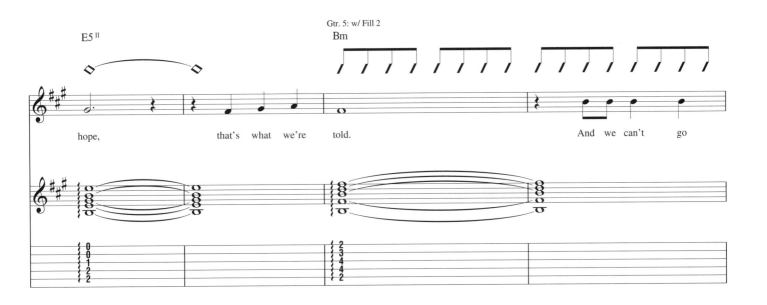

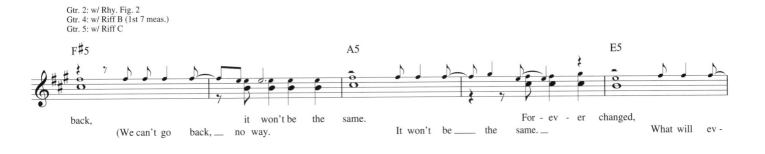

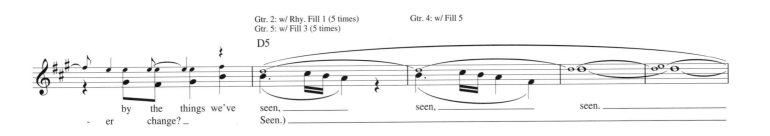

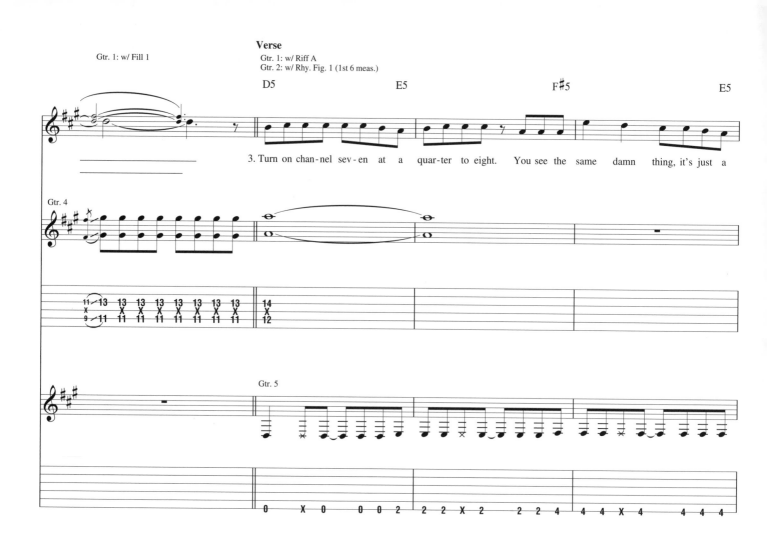

Mountain

Words and Music by Benji Madden, Joel Madden and Billy Martin

Drop D tuning, down 1/2 step:
(low to high) Db-Ab-Db-Gb-Bb-Eb

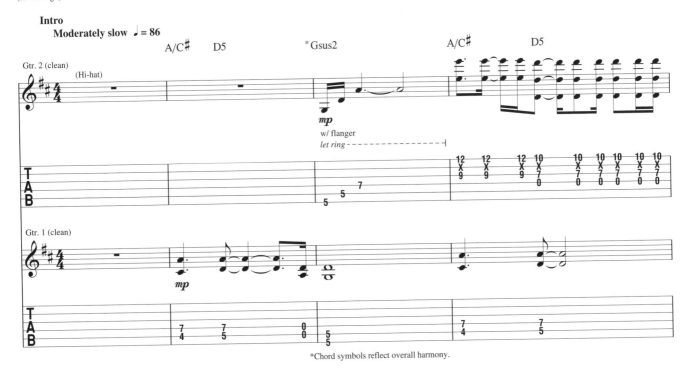

*Chord symbols reflect overall harmony.

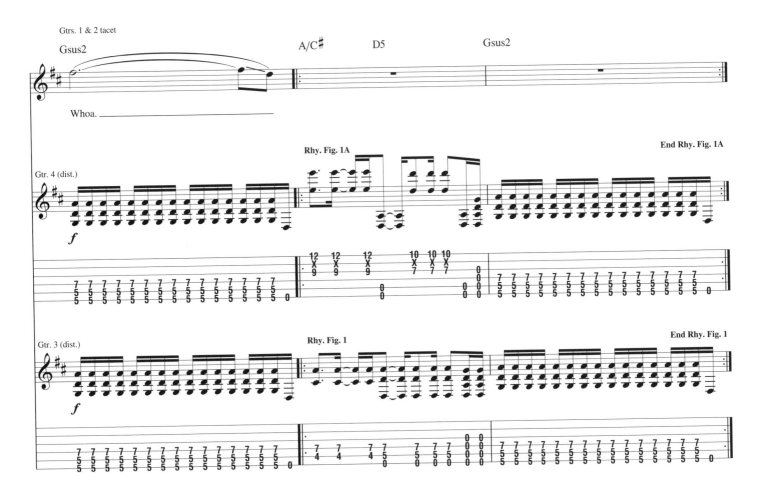

Verse

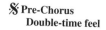

give up ev - 'ry - thing___ and I'd___ for - get it.___ I

was - n't___ on___ a moun - tain when it___ came___ to

me.___ All my___ life's___ been wast - ed___

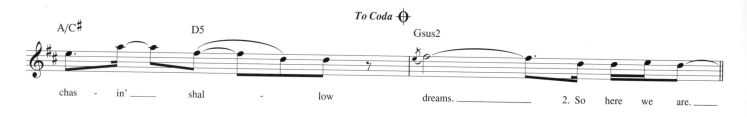

chas - in' ____ shal - low dreams. ____ 2. So here we are. ____

Verse

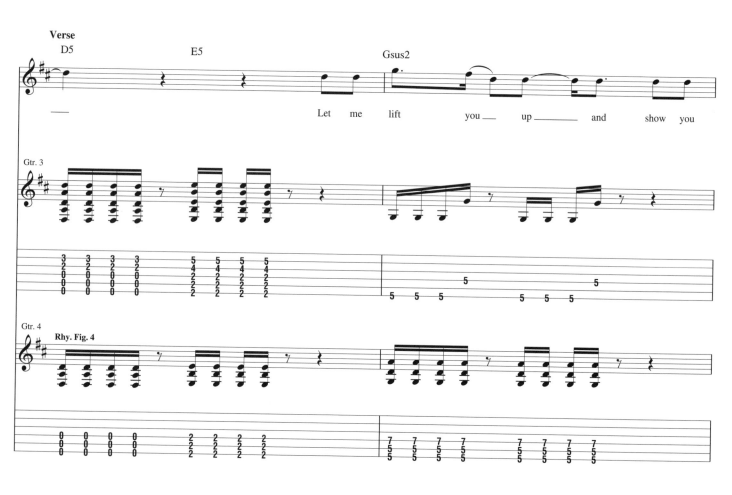

Let me lift you ____ up ____ and show you

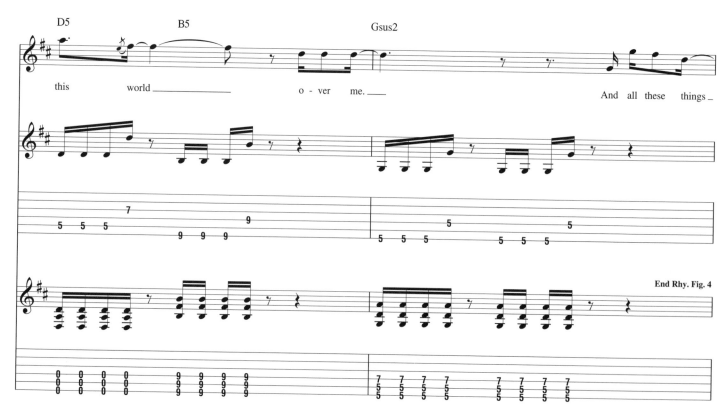

this world ____ o - ver me. ____ And all these things ____

what I've gained __ and what I've seen, __ it can't com-pare __ to the love __

D.S. al Coda

that you could give to me. ____ So

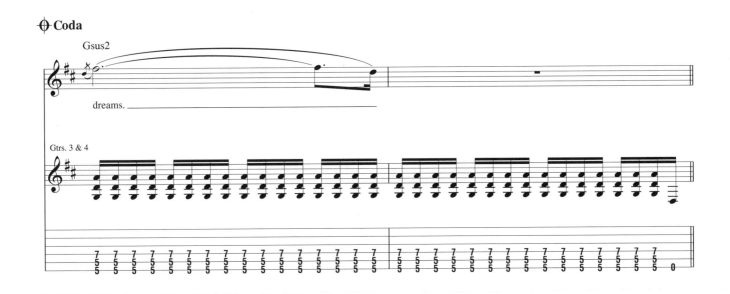

Coda

dreams. ____

Gtrs. 3 & 4: w/ Rhy. Figs. 5 & 5A

All this time, — I thought that I — gained ev - 'ry - thing. — If

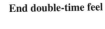

End double-time feel

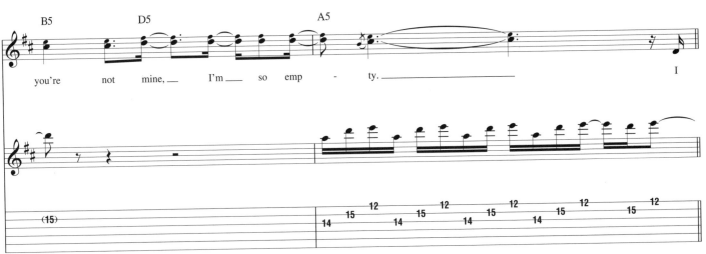

you're not mine, — I'm — so emp - ty. — I

Chorus

Gtr. 1: w/ Rhy. Fig. 3 (3 1/2 times)
Gtr. 2: w/ Riff B (3 1/2 times)

Gtr. 6 tacet

was - n't — on — a moun - tain when it came, — when it — came to me. —

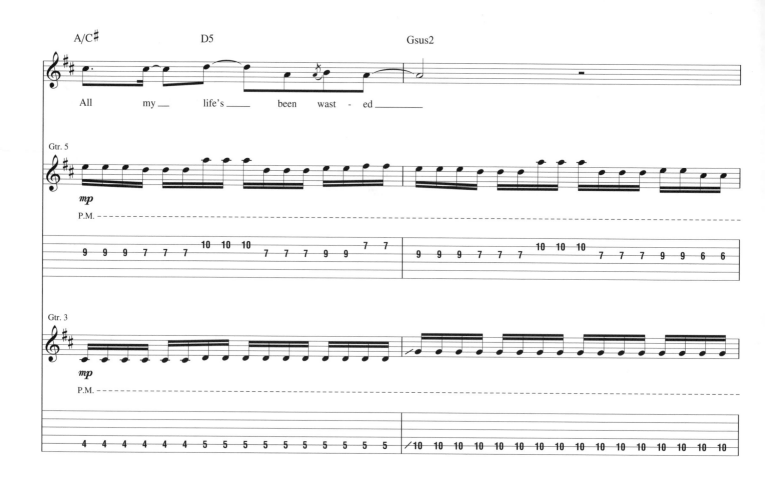

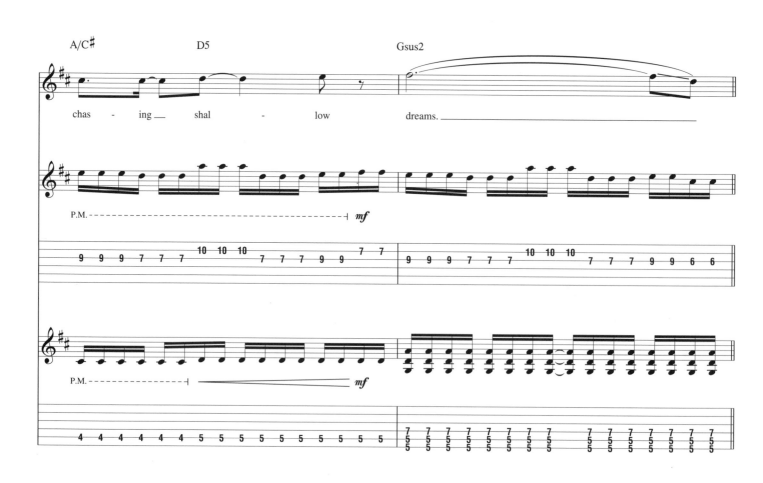

Interlude

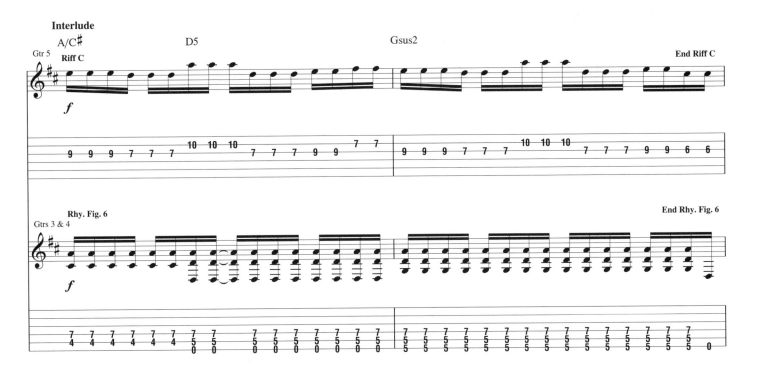

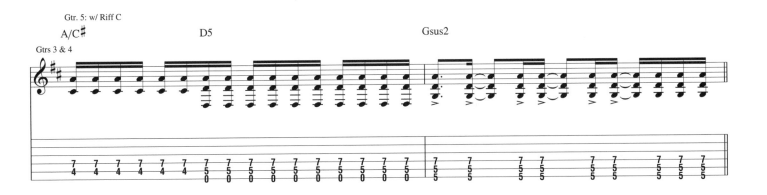

Gtr. 5: w/ Riff C

Outro

Gtrs. 3 & 4: w/ Rhy. Fig. 6 (2 times)
Gtr. 5: w/ Riff C (2 times)

So please come back to me, I'm right here wait - ing.

So please come back to me a - gain.

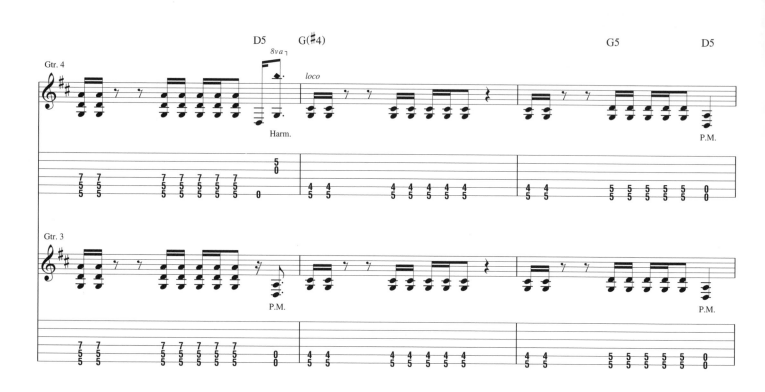

We Believe

Words and Music by Benji Madden and Joel Madden

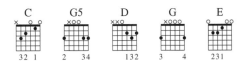

Tune down 1/2 step:
(low to high) E♭-A♭-D♭-G♭-B♭-E♭

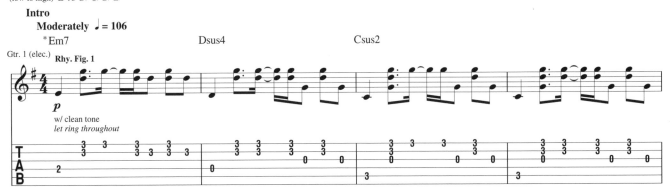

*Chord symbols reflect implied harmony.

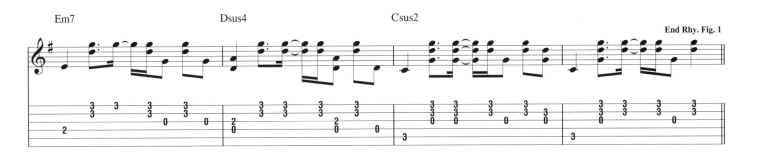

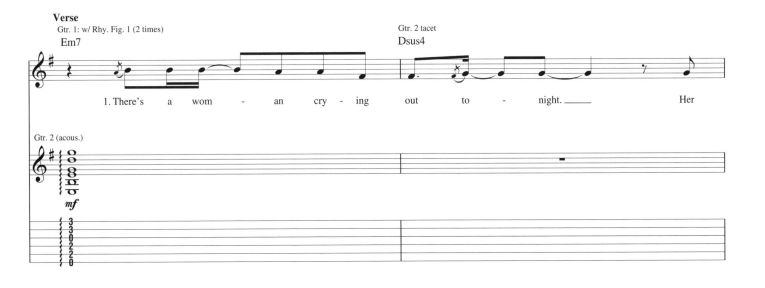

*Delay set for dotted eighth-note regeneration w/ 7 repeats.

D

we be - lieve, _____ in this _____ love. _____
in this _____ love.) _

C

End Rhy. Fig. 3

(cont. in notation)

End Rhy. Fig. 3A

End Riff A

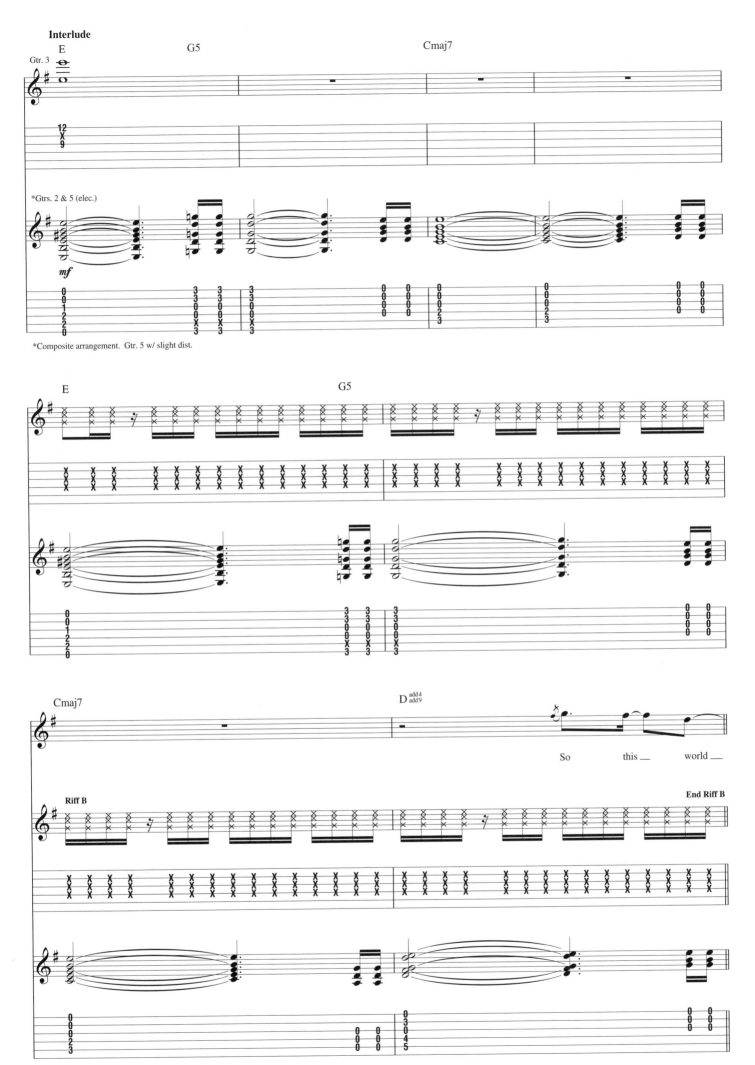

So this __ this __ world __

Chorus

Gtrs. 2 & 4: w/ Rhy. Figs. 3 & 3A
Gtr. 3: w/ Riff A (1st 6 meas.)
Gtr. 5 tacet

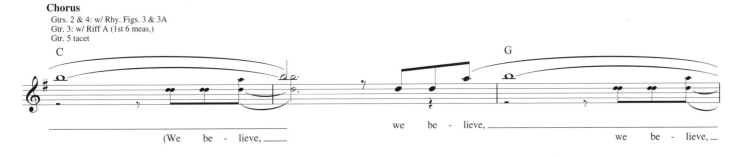

(We be - lieve, ____ we be - lieve, ____ we be - lieve, __

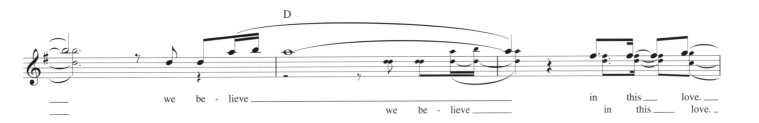

__ we be - lieve ____ in this __ love.
__ we be - lieve ____ in this __ love. __

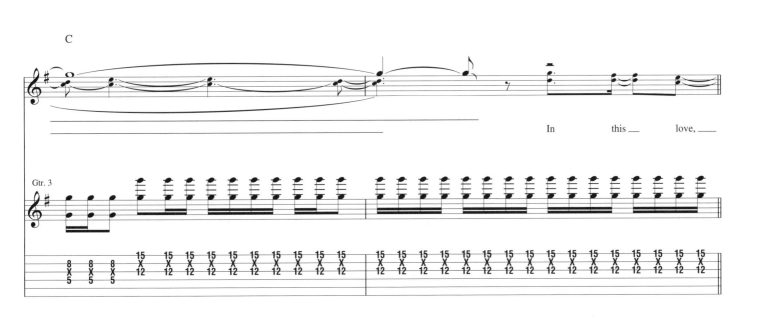

In this __ love, __

Outro-Chorus

We be - lieve, ____ in this __ love, __

we be - lieve, _____ in this ___ love, ___

we be - lieve _____ in this ___ love. ___
in this ___ love.) _

(w/ delay repeats)

It Wasn't Enough

Words and Music by Benji Madden, Joel Madden and John Feldmann

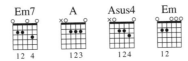

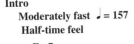

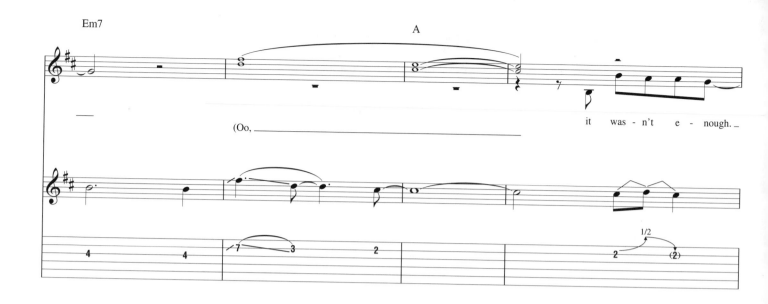

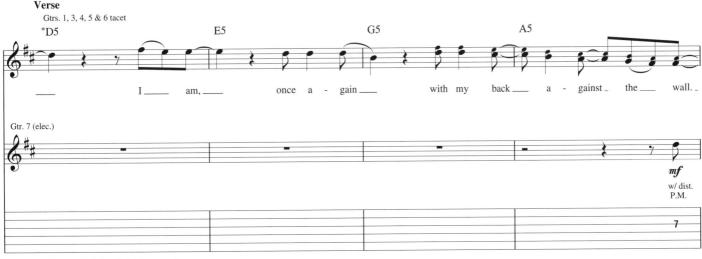

*Chord symbols implied by bass, next 8 meas.

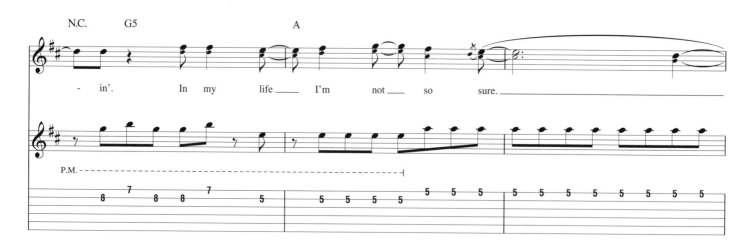

Chorus
Half-time feel

Gtrs. 1 & 5: w/ Rhy. Fig. 3 (3 1/2 times)
Gtrs. 3 & 4: w/ Rhy. Fig. 3A (3 1/2 times)
Gtr. 6: w/ Riff A
Gtr. 7 tacet

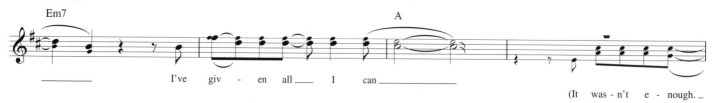

Outro-Chorus

I've giv - en all___ I can.___ It was - n't e - nough___

Gtrs. 1 & 3: w/ Rhy. Figs. 6 & 6A

Em   *Aadd9

to keep___ you in___ my hand.___ Should I give up?___

*Chord symbols reflect combined harmony.

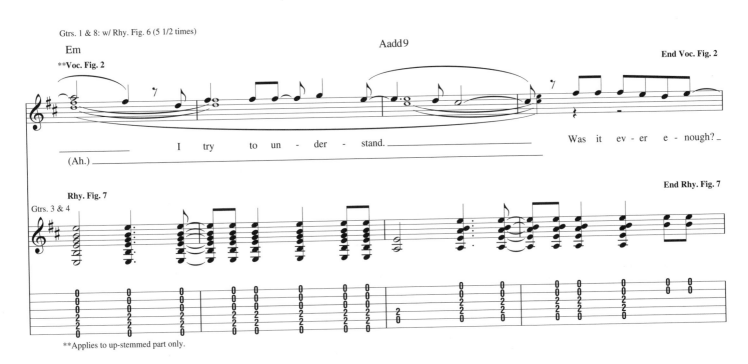

Gtrs. 1 & 8: w/ Rhy. Fig. 6 (5 1/2 times)

Em   Aadd9   End Voc. Fig. 2

**Voc. Fig. 2

I try to un - der - stand.___ Was it ev - er e - nough?___

(Ah.)

End Rhy. Fig. 7

Rhy. Fig. 7

Gtrs. 3 & 4

**Applies to up-stemmed part only.

Gtrs. 3 & 4: w/ Rhy. Fig. 7 (4 1/2 times)

— I don't un - der - stand. _____

Bkgd. Voc.: w/ Voc. Fig. 2 (4 times)

Ev - 'ry - thing __ you want __ from me, __ I've fought so hard for ev - 'ry - thing. __

Ev - 'ry - thing __ you want __ from me, __ I've tried so hard, could nev - er be. __

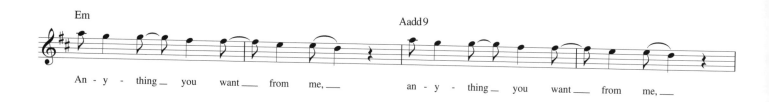

An - y - thing __ you want __ from me, __ an - y - thing __ you want __ from me, __

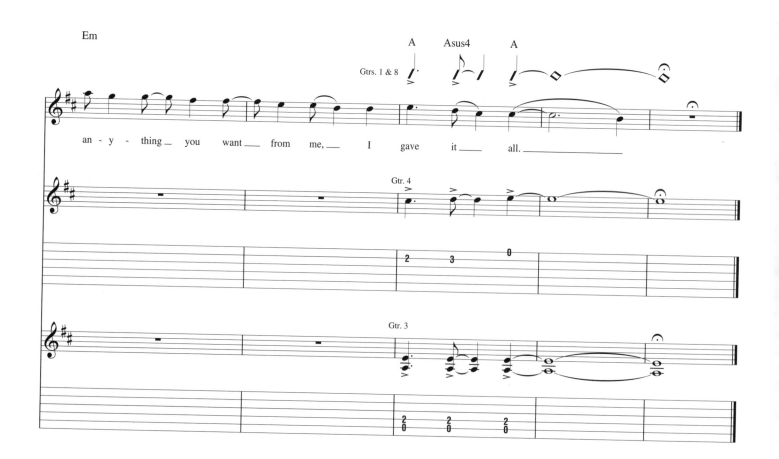

an - y - thing __ you want __ from me, __ I gave it __ all. _____

In This World (Murder)

Words and Music by Benji Madden and Joel Madden

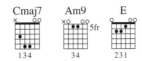

Tune down 1/2 step:
(low to high) E♭-A♭-D♭-G♭-B♭-E♭

Intro

Moderately slow ♩. = 68

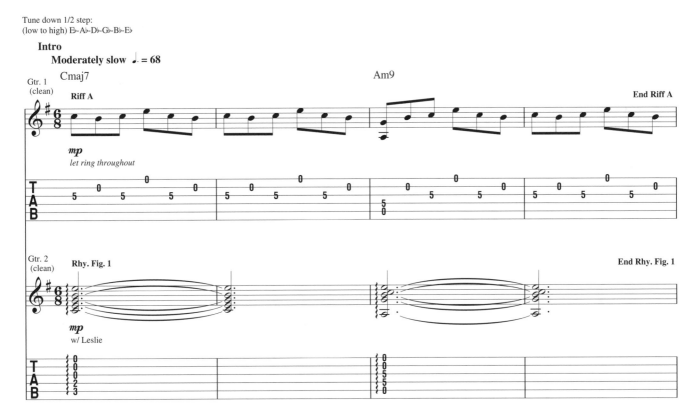

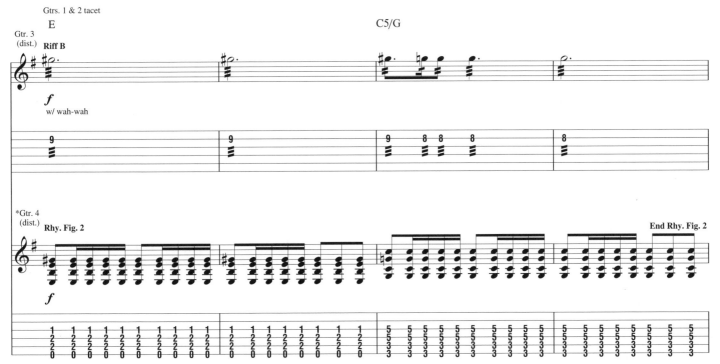

*Doubled throughout

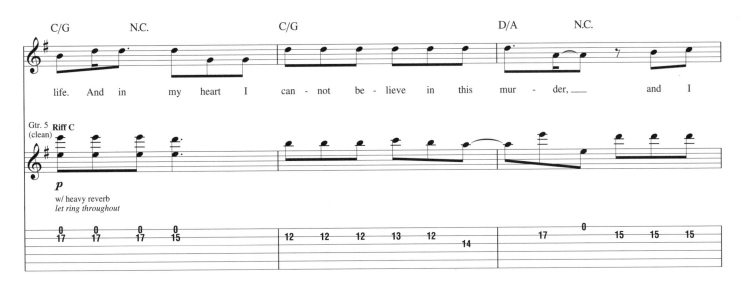

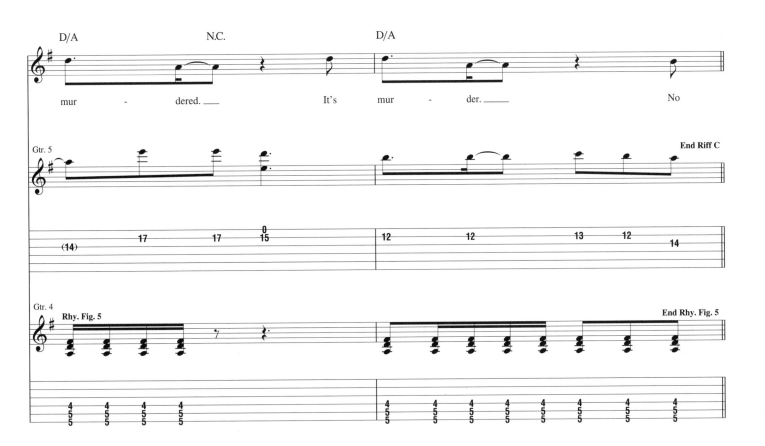

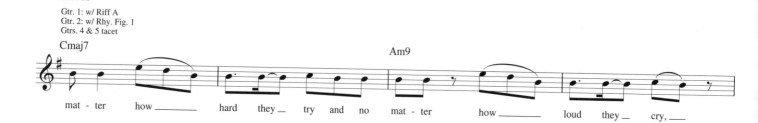

Verse

Gtr. 4: w/ Rhy. Fig. 4 (3 1/2 times)
Gtr. 3 tacet

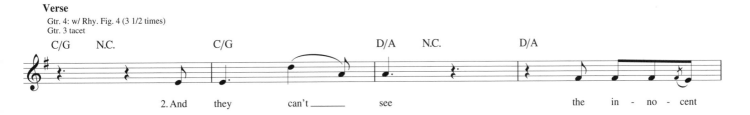

2. And they can't _____ see   the in - no - cent

lives,   the point - less suf - fer - ing. _____

Gtr. 5: w/ Riff C

And in my heart I wan - na un - do all this mur - der ___ and give back the in - no - cent

Gtr. 4: w/ Rhy. Fig. 5

life. O - pen cag - es and stop their lux - u - ri - ous mur - der. ___ It's mur - der. ___ No

Chorus

Gtr. 1: w/ Riff A

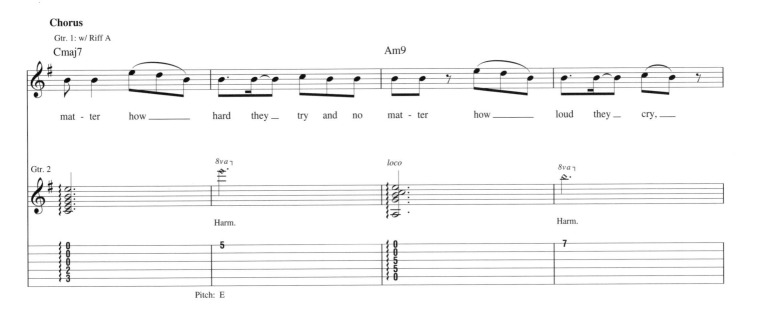

mat - ter how _____ hard they ___ try and no mat - ter how _____ loud they ___ cry, ___

Gtr. 3: w/ Riff B
Gtr. 4: w/ Rhy. Fig. 2

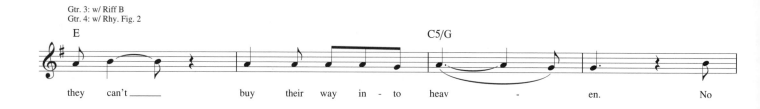

they can't _____ buy their way in - to heav - en. No

Gtr. 4: w/ Rhy. Fig. 3

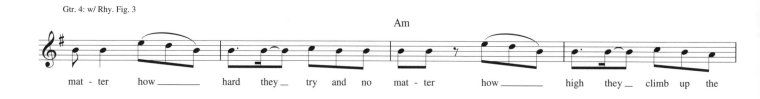

mat - ter how _____ hard they _ try and no mat - ter how _____ high they _ climb up the

Gtr. 4: w/ Rhy. Fig. 2

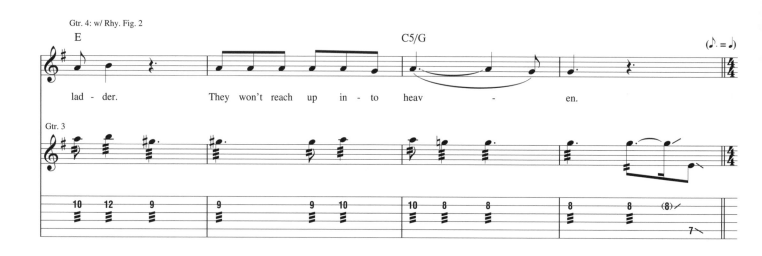

lad - der. They won't reach up in - to heav - en.

Gtr. 3

Interlude

Gtr. 3 tacet

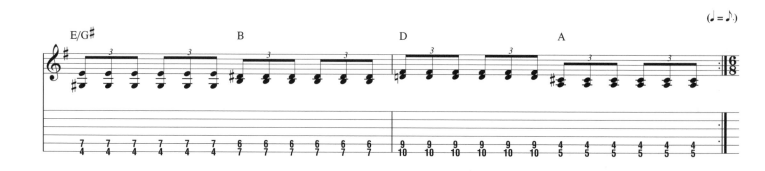

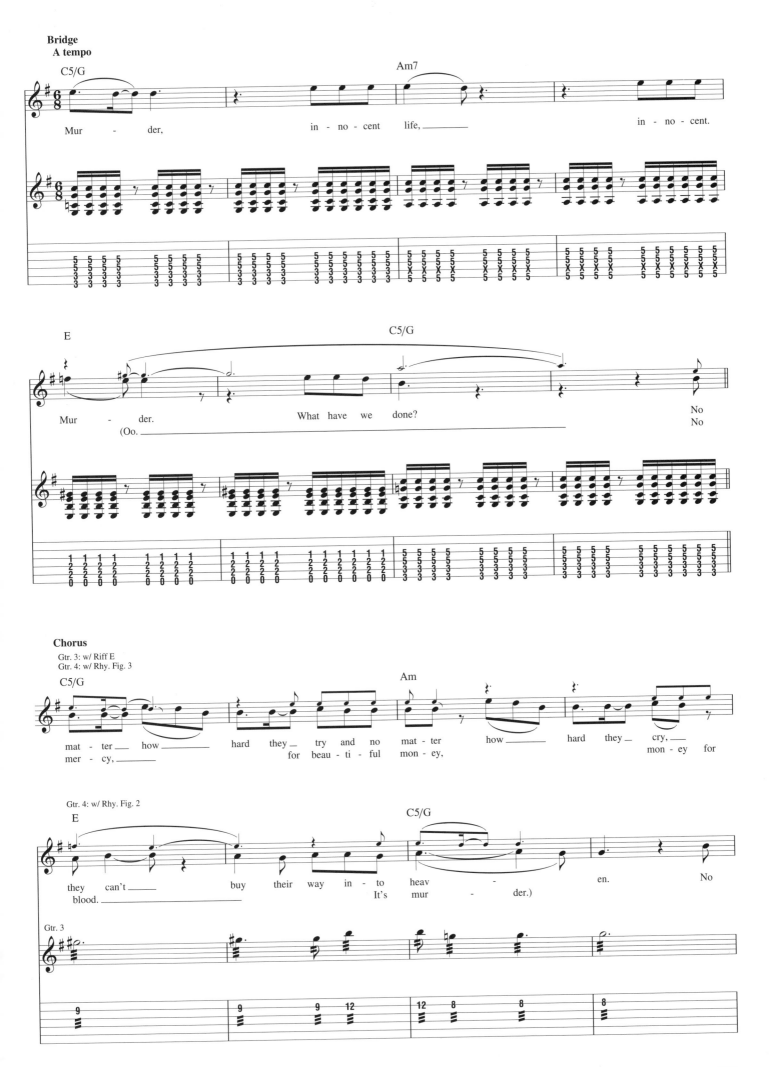

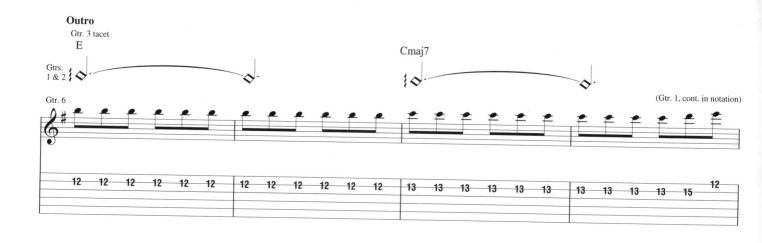

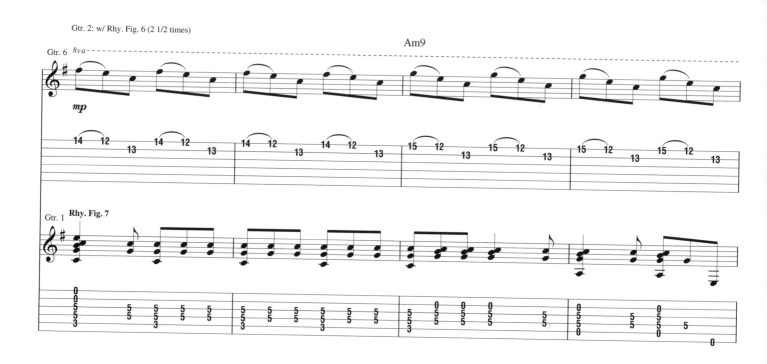

Am9

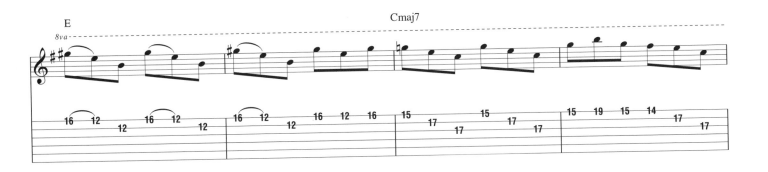

E   Cmaj7

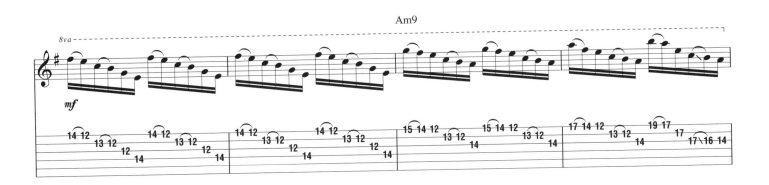

Am9

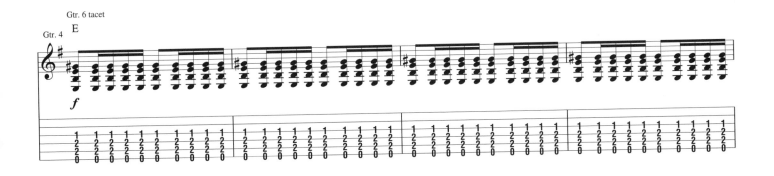

Gtr. 6 tacet
Gtr. 4 E

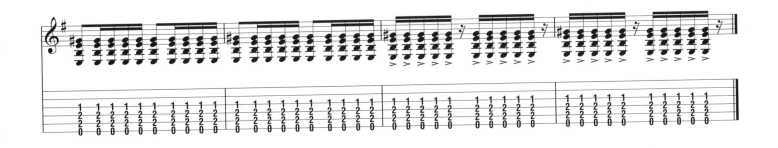

Falling Away

Words and Music by Benji Madden and Joel Madden

Tune down 1/4 step

Gtr. 3: Drop D tuning, down 1/4 step:
(low to high) D-A-D-G-B-E
(Calibrate tuner to A = 425 Hz.)

Intro
Moderately fast ♩ = 140

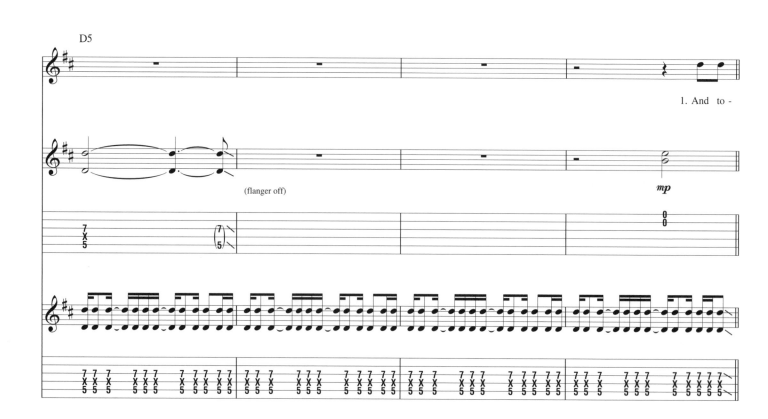

𝄋 Chorus

Gtr. 1: w/ Rhy. Fig. 1 (2 times)
Gtr. 2: w/ Riff A (2 times)

I feel you fall-in' a-way, feel you fall-in' a-way, feel you fall-in' a-way ___ from me a-gain.

To Coda ⊕

I feel you fall-in' a-way, feel you fall-in' a-way, feel you fall-in' a-way ___ from me a-gain.

1.

Interlude

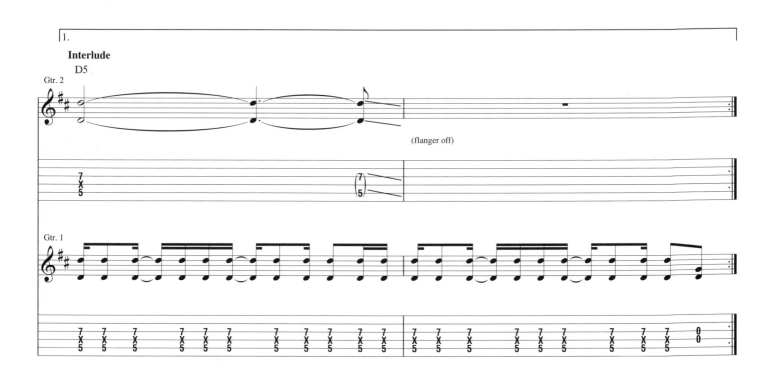

(flanger off)

2.

Chorus

Gtr. 1: w/ Rhy. Fig. 1 (2 times)
Gtr. 2: w/ Riff A (2 times)

I feel you fall-in' a-way, feel you fall-in' a-way, feel you fall-in' a-way ___ from me a-gain.

I feel you fall-in' a-way, feel you fall-in' a-way, feel you fall-in' a-way ___ from me a-gain.

Bridge

F#5 E5 D5 E5   F#5   A   F#5 E5 D5 E5   F#5   G5

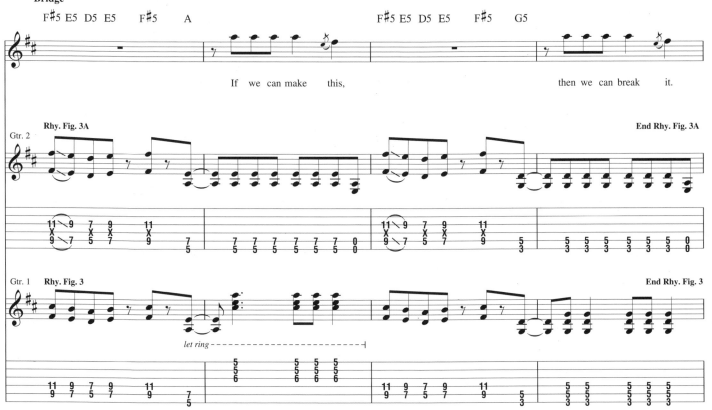

If we can make this,   then we can break it.

D.S. al Coda

Gtrs. 1 & 2: w/ Rhy. Figs. 3 & 3A

F#5 E5 D5 E5   F#5   A   F#5 E5 D5 E5   F#5 G5   A5

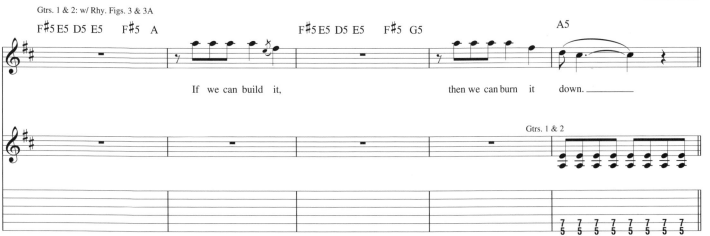

If we can build it,   then we can burn it down. _____

Gtrs. 1 & 2

Coda

N.C.

I feel you fall-in' a-way,   feel you fall-in' a-way,   feel you fall-in' a-way ___ from me ___ a-gain.

*Fade in, next 4 meas. w/ tone filter sweep & dist.

Outro-Chorus

Meet My Maker

Words and Music by Benji Madden and Joel Madden

Tune down 1/2 step:
(low to high) E♭-A♭-D♭-G♭-B♭-E♭

Intro
Moderately ♩ = 103

This is the way I meet _____ my mak - er to - night.

*Fade in, next 2 meas. w/ tone filter sweep

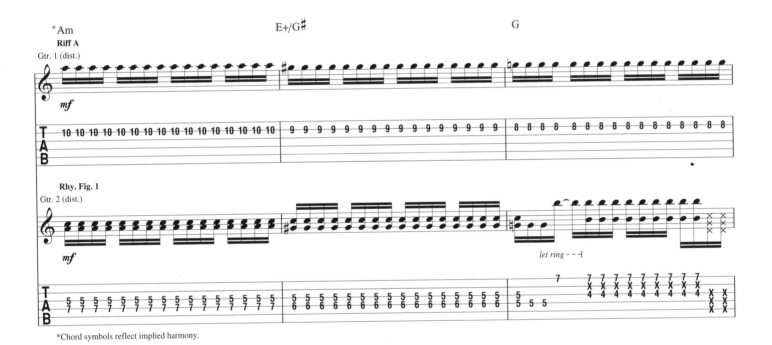

*Chord symbols reflect implied harmony.

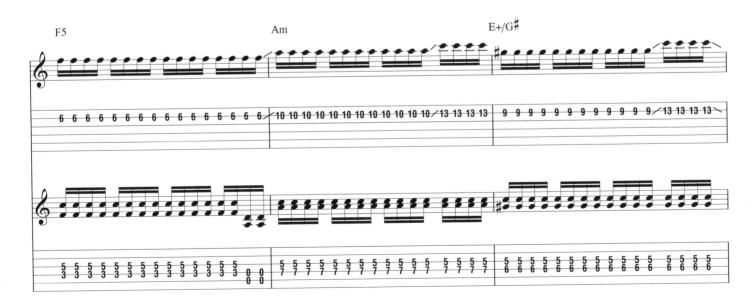

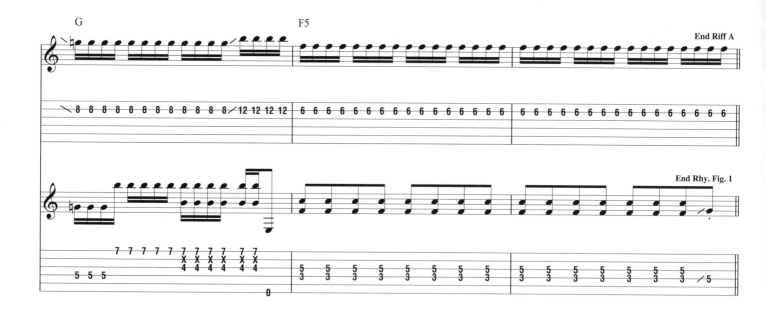

Verse

Gtrs. 1 & 2 tacet

1. So this is it. ___ This is my life. ___ This is my time, ___ it's end - ing to - night.

I made my mis - takes. ___ I tried to live right. ___ Stepped out of the dark - ness in - to the light. ___

Gtr. 3: w/ Riff B
Gtr. 4: w/ Riff B1 (3 times)

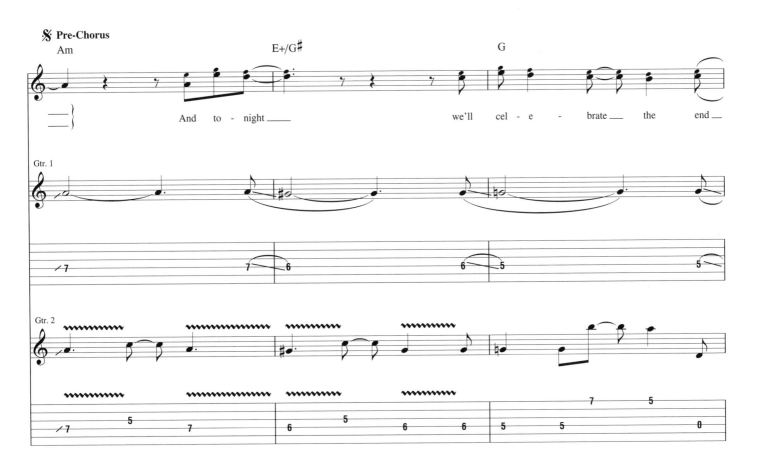

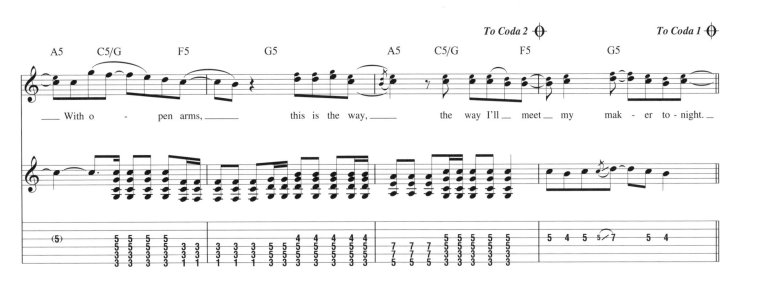

With o - pen arms, _____ this is the way, _____ the way I'll _____ meet _____ my mak - er to - night. _____

Interlude

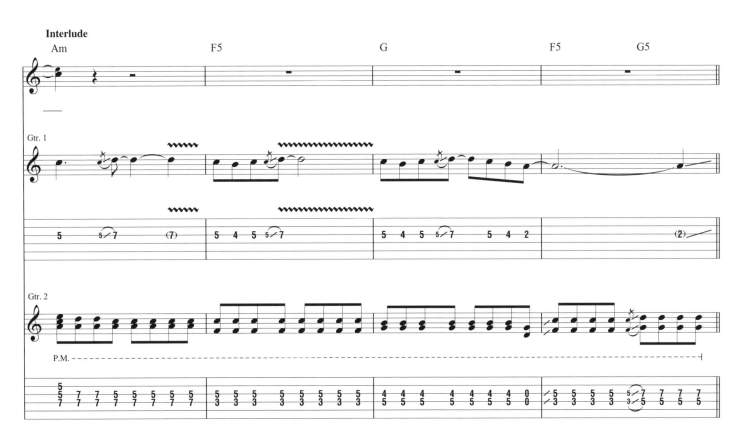

Verse

Gtr. 1 tacet
Gtr. 3: w/ Riff B

2. And on my grave _____ what will it say? _____ Here lies an - oth - er soul _____ that we saved. _____

Riff D   **End Riff D**

Gtr. 2

So please don't cry.___ Sleep at___ night___ and I will___ wait___ on the oth - er side.___

Coda 1

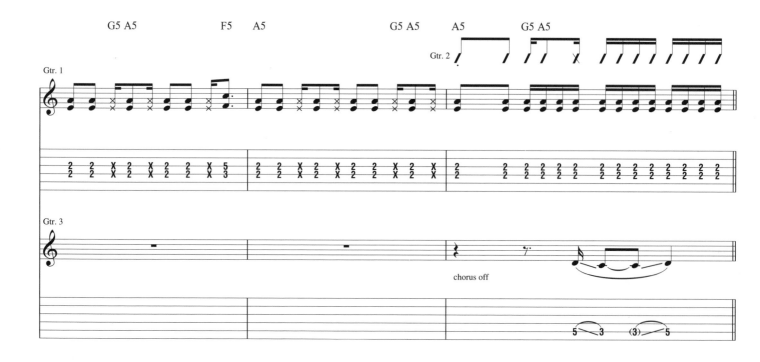

Bridge

Gtr. 1: w/ Riff A
Gtr. 2: w/ Rhy. Fig. 1
Gtr. 3 tacet

And to - night ____ we'll cel - e - brate ____ the end _____

D.S.S. al Coda 2

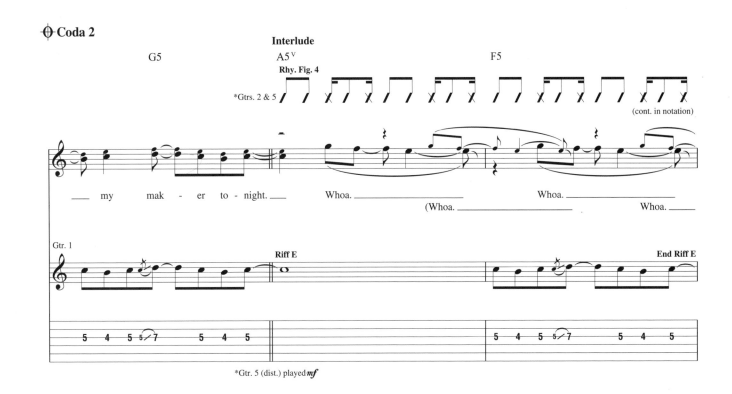

of this life. ____ And we'll sing, _____ hee, yeah, hee, yeah, hee, yeah, hee, yeah. ____

⊕ **Coda 2**

Interlude

____ my mak - er to - night. ____ Whoa. Whoa. Whoa.
(Whoa. _____) Whoa.

*Gtr. 5 (dist.) played *mf**

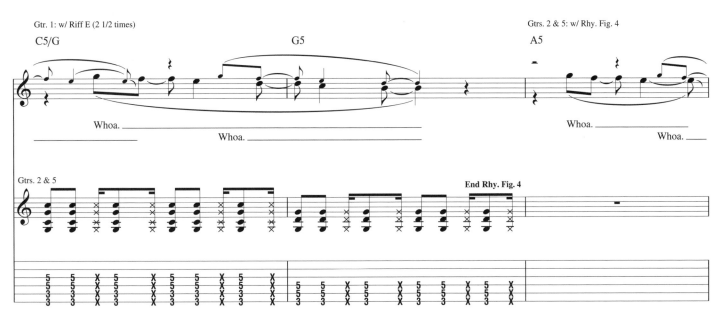

Gtr. 1: w/ Riff E (2 1/2 times)   Gtrs. 2 & 5: w/ Rhy. Fig. 4

C5/G   G5   A5

Whoa. Whoa. Whoa. Whoa.

Gtrs. 2 & 5   End Rhy. Fig. 4

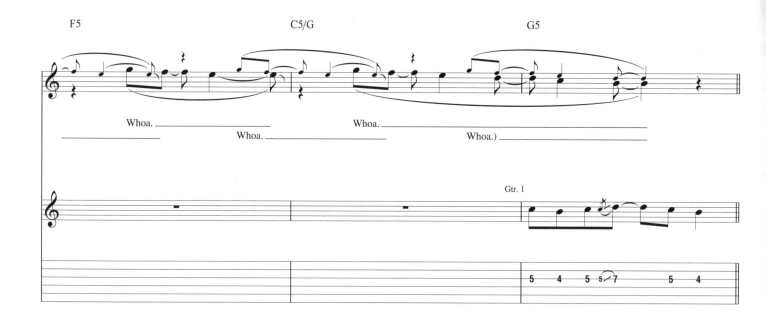

Outro

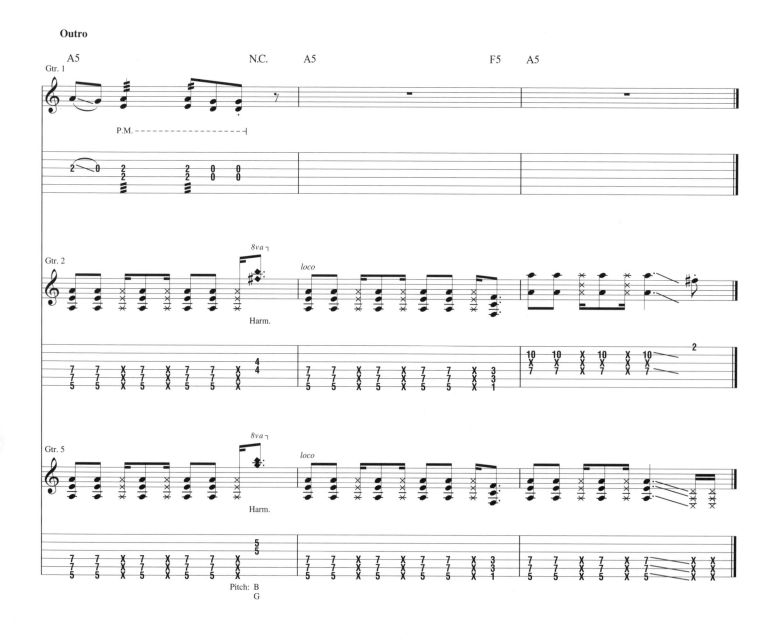